Web3 The dezentralized Revolution on the Internet

Daniel Müller

Published by Dezentrale Ltd., 2024.

While every precaution has been taken in the preparation of this book, the publisher assumes no responsibility for errors or omissions, or for damages resulting from the use of the information contained herein.

WEB3 THE DEZENTRALIZED REVOLUTION ON THE INTERNET

First edition. February 22, 2024.

ISBN: 979-8224888467

Written by Daniel Müller.

The Internet is just hype

Bill Gates, 1995 Founder Microsoft

I think there may be a market for five computers in the world

Thomas Watson. 1943 CEO IBM

There is no reason why everyone should have a computer at home

Ken Olsen 1977 Founder of digital Equipment Corp.

Table of Contents

The Subject

Web3, is a buzzword that keeps cropping up in the mainstream media.

Sometimes with sensational news about the prices achieved by NFTs. 69 million US dollars for Beepl's Everydays, 6 million US dollars for a CryptoPunk and a few more.

However, NFTs, non-fungible tokens, are only one aspect of Web3, important, no question, but they are not Web3. With this book, I would like to introduce you to Web3.

I will explain the difference to WEB 2.0 and take a short detour into today's currency system.

What for?

The oldest application on the Web3 is Bitcoin. Bitcoin is a counter-proposal to the current currency system and aims to replace the weaknesses and injustices inherent in the system.

To understand Bitcoin and the Web3, it is essential to know the current system, only then is it possible to grasp the unimagined possibilities and draw your own conclusions.

The blockchain is the underlying technology of Bitcoin, which plays an essential role in Web3 and makes things possible that were previously impossible.

Of course, in this book, you will also learn about the concept of a blockchain and how it basically works. I can reassure you at this point that this will not be a digression into cryptography and mathematics. Nor will I bore you with technical details. It is important to me that you understand the concept, and that is possible without formulas and technical terms.

I will then introduce you to the various applications that are already being used in Web3. These include NFTs, DeFi, decentralized financial applications, DAOs,

decentralized autonomous organizations and, of course, the metaverse, the virtual worlds.

I would also like to introduce you to some blockchain applications that are used in real life. These applications can automate and simplify various processes in the business world.

Web 1.0, Web 2.0, Web 3.0, Web3

In this chapter, I would like to explain the differences between these three Internet eras.

Web 1.0 Read

WEB 1.0 is commonly referred to as the beginnings of the Internet.

At that time, users could only actually read. In other words, you could view texts on the websites. It didn't matter whether it was news, instructions, or research results on a wide variety of topics.

It was not possible to interact with these websites. Social media as we know it today was therefore not possible.

Web 2.0 Reading and Writing

WEB 2.0 is the term we use to describe today's Internet.

Today, it is possible to interact with websites. This began with the forerunners of today's social media, continued with the opportunity of uploading images and videos, and also made it possible to process payments via third-party providers. WEB 2.0 also marked the birth of online commerce.

At this point, it is important to understand that centralized institutions are always involved in payment processing.

I would like to cite PayPal as an example here. PayPal debits the amount from the buyer's bank account or credit/debit card and sends the amount, minus a processing fee, to the seller's account. In very simplified terms, as the amount can also be temporarily stored on PayPal.

This means that at least three centralized institutions are always involved in these transactions. The buyer's bank, PayPal, and the seller's bank.

Why do I pay particular attention to this?

It works differently in Web3, more on that later. In WEB 2.0, you always interact with a centralized company. Be it the social media platform, an online retailer, your bank and possibly offers from the government.

This contains some advantages, but also many disadvantages.

Advantages

You always have a contact person.

If you lose or forget your access data, you will receive new access data. If there were problems with a bank transfer, you can contact the relevant bank. If a delivery is faulty, can you contact the retailer and complain about the goods.

I think you can see what I'm getting at — you are relieved of almost all responsibility, and you almost always have someone to help you out if you mess something up, in terms of access to data.

Disadvantages

The biggest disadvantage is probably your data.

With every website and every service you want to use, you have to disclose data about yourself. Depending on the service you wish to use, this can range from your name and e-mail address to your address, telephone number, bank account and tax number.

The fact that this data is often not stored securely or is even traded with is nothing new. In addition, you pay for every service you use. The fees charged by the payment processor, bank charges, subscription fees and much more.

If you think that if an offer costs nothing, it is free, I have to disappoint you. In such cases, you pay with your data. Have you ever wondered why company XY is contacting you?

This is the price you pay for a supposedly free offer on WEB 2.0.

The biggest problem, however, lies in the dependency on these institutions. Your bank balance can be frozen at any time. A payment service provider can block your account at any time.

In October 2022, parts of PayPal's new terms and conditions appeared online, leading to mass account terminations and putting the share price under severe pressure. This was triggered by PayPal's statement that it would withhold up to 2,500 US dollars in penalties if the account holder disseminated opinions online that contradicted PayPal's views.

In the real world, this is called censorship. PayPal immediately rowed back and explained that this was never the intention.

Almost identical things happened during the truck strikes in Canada. Bank and PayPal accounts of the striking truck drivers were frozen. The same applied to supporters of the strikes. Anyone who supported the strikes financially had to expect their bank accounts to be blocked.

Web3 Read, Write, Transfer Values

I would like to start by saying that there are different views on Web 3.0 and Web3.

Some describe Web 3.0 as a technical extension of Web 2.0. Cloud computing, SaaS (Software as a Service), logging in via your Google account and many other new applications, such as the Internet of Things, which are based on Web 2.0, are considered Web 3.0.

Web 3 describes the decentralized approach.

Others equate Web 3.0 with Web3.

I prefer the distinction between Web 3.0 and Web3. I can't tell you what is right or wrong. My point is that you have heard this once to clarify things.

Depending on where you obtain information from, the terms can have different meanings.

The transfer of values is now added to the characteristics of WEB 2.0.

Centralized institutions such as banks or payment processors are no longer necessary. These transactions are peer-to-peer, i.e., from user to user. This is comparable to cash payments.

You receive the goods and pay with cash, again without the need for a third party.

For the first time, Web3 makes it possible to clearly prove ownership of digital assets. This doesn't just have to be cryptocurrencies; it works for any digital and real value.

What's more, it doesn't matter how high the amount to be sent is. If you want to transfer 100,000, the fee is just as high as if you only would like to transfer 100.

Depending on the blockchain, we are talking about cent amounts.

The registration or use of services is also entirely different. You link your digital wallet, which contains your authorization, usually in the form of an NFT or in the form of your personal data. In the case of an NFT, the use of the offer can be completely anonymous. When it comes to your data, it remains in your digital wallet and is only checked but not saved.

This also results in advantages and disadvantages.

Advantages

You are and remain the owner of your data.

You decide which data you wish to disclose and which you do not. If the desired offer is activated via NFTs, you can use the offer anonymously. I will go into NFTs and decentralized identities in much more detail later.

I hope you can still follow my explanations.

A centralized third party is no longer required for value transactions. This means that for now, nobody knows how much you have transferred to whom. Later in the book, you will see why I wrote "for now".

More transparency than on a blockchain is hardly possible. You may already be aware that the Web3 gives you back your privacy, restricts access from outside and does not require any control instances. At least not necessarily.

That sounds very positive, but it also has disadvantages.

Disadvantages

Since centralized institutions are no longer necessary, no one can help you if you lose your account access data.

If that happens, your money is gone. More precisely, it's still there, but you no longer have access to it. The same applies to your NFTs and your digital identity. Whereby you can get your identity back, but it can be a bit of a hassle.

In short, if you lose the access data to your digital wallet, you have a serious problem.

By extension, this means that Web3 requires a high degree of personal responsibility.

This is the price you pay for your privacy and the freedom that comes with it. We will see later in the book that there are of course also hybrid solutions.

There you can delegate your responsibility to third parties.

Today's Monetary System

Let's now take a look at how today's monetary system works.

I'm not going to delve into the infinite depths. Here, too, I would like to explain the concept to you without using fancy formulas and technical terms.

Why do I think it is important to explain the existing currency system?

The first Web3 application, Bitcoin, is basically the antithesis of today's currencies. To understand the idea behind it, it is necessary to know the system behind our currencies. I am not trying to proselytize, but to show you the two systems.

You can only form your opinion if you are familiar with both approaches.

Money

Foremost, we need to define what money actually is and what characteristics money must have.

Means of Exchange and Payment:

Money is used to settle debts.

To this end, it is necessary for money to be accepted by all economic participants. Acceptance is either voluntary or coercive. In the case of voluntary acceptance, the market participants have agreed on a commodity which they accept as a means of payment. Money that must be accepted by force is all state currencies.

In this case, the state specifies which money may be used and which the state accepts for the payment of taxes and duties.

Store of Value:

Money must serve as a store of value and therefore must not lose its purchasing power over time.

Calculation Unit:

Money is used by market participants as a vehicle for setting prices. With the help of money, the value of a good can be depicted, making it possible to compare goods with each other via the price.

Divisible:

Money must be divided into smaller units.

€1 corresponds to 100-euro cents. There are also some practical aspects.

Money should be durable, easy to transport and forgery-proof. I will go into two points in more detail below.

I would like to show you the impact of supposedly small changes. I would also like to show you the difference between money and currencies.

Means of Exchange and Payment

In this section, I would like to show you the effects that occur when a means of payment is introduced by coercion and not on a voluntary basis. It is not relevant whether this means of payment is a gold coin or paper. The effects are always the same.

Voluntary

Let us assume that in our example, gold coins are used as a means of payment that were not introduced by coercion.

What would happen if the issuer of the coins or other fraudulent market participants started to manipulate the gold coins?

They mix another cheaper metal into the gold, copper, for example.

This allows the players to produce more coins with the same amount of gold, as the missing gold is replaced by copper. This reduces the gold content in the coins and thus the value of the coin.

In addition, this manipulation puts more coins into circulation, as they are no longer 100% gold. This is called inflation, from the Latin "inflare" to inflate.

The consequence of this inflation is a loss of purchasing power of the respective coins.

Now let's look at what would happen to market participants when they realize the hoax.

The first reaction will be to raise prices, as the original prices were based on the assumption of 100% gold in the coin. This is known as consumer price rise. If the fraudulent market participants overdo it with the addition of copper, these coins are no longer accepted as a means of payment, become worthless and are discarded.

They are replaced by other gold coins made of 100% gold.

The same applies if confidence in a means of payment is lost. It is not relevant whether it is gold coins, paper money or cigarettes.

It can be concluded from this that in the case of voluntary acceptance, the high-quality or trustworthy means of payment are always in circulation. The bad money is discarded.

Compulsion

Now let's look at what happens when acceptance is enforced by the state.

The assumption is the same as above, only we replace voluntariness with coercion.

The market participants must pay their taxes and duties with the compulsory means of payment. This means that they cannot switch to other means of payment at this time.

If the state begins to add copper to its gold coins, thereby inflating the amount of currency in circulation, prices will rise again.

In this case, too, the original prices were based on the assumption of 100% gold in the coins.

If the state overdoes it with the addition of copper, the opposite of voluntary acceptance will happen.

Market participants will take the good coins with a high gold content out of circulation and hoard them.

As a result, only the low-quality coins that no longer enjoy trust will be in circulation.

In addition, parallel markets will develop in which voluntarily accepted means of payment will re-establish themselves.

This means that compulsory means of payment will only be used to pay taxes and duties, and here too only the least valuable ones. Everything else is settled with the voluntary means of payment that the market participants have agreed on.

This can be observed in all countries where the national currency is losing value. Citizens are switching to the US dollar, for example.

The introduction of a compulsory means of payment therefore has far-reaching consequences for market participants and the state itself.

The state's revenue will always be the least valuable means of payment in the event of a loss of confidence.

In addition, markets are created outside legal tender, which further damages the state.

Store of Value

Storing values over time is an essential and necessary property.

To give you a more profound understanding of this, allow me to make the following assumption:

A fisherman goes out to sea in his boat at sunrise and fishes all day. In the evening, he takes his boat back to the harbor to sell his catch.

Now let's take a look at the values and goods involved. There are the goods he needs for his work. The boat, nets, and fuel that he requires for fishing. He also uses his time and labor to catch fish with the goods. The catch thus reflects the values and goods used.

In the evening, he sells his catch for, say, 1000. The catch thus receives a price. The 1000 now represents the resources and values used.

For an office worker, a production employee or a sales clerk, the monthly salary therefore reflects the time spent and the work performed.

When our test subjects mentioned above go to the supermarket and do their shopping, they exchange part of their expended resources and values for the expended resources and values of the supermarket owner.

To achieve this, they use a means of payment that stores the services rendered by the owner.

If the means of payment used is not a store of value, this has unpleasant consequences.

This subsequently reduces the value of the service.

Put simply, the service, the time, and the goods used are worth less today. Purchasing power is dwindling.

Conversely, the use of goods and values must be higher today to maintain the same purchasing power.

As you can see, it is essential that a means of payment fulfills its function as a store of value.

Today's currencies have long since ceased to function as a store of value. That is why we cannot actually speak of money in the true sense of the word. Rather, they are currencies that are still used as a unit of account and medium of exchange, but no longer fulfill the function of a store of value.

Now that we have noticed that our current means of payment are not money, but currencies, let's take a look at how they are created.

Fiat Currencies

Fiat currencies are derived from the Latin word for "let there be". Fiat lux, let there be light, as can already be read in the Bible.

A distinction is made between two types of currency.

The central bank currency and the book or Giro currency.

The central bank currency is issued by the central banks and comprises the cash, coins, and notes in circulation. Except for cash, central bank currency only circulates within the banking sector.

The central bank is the bank of the commercial banks. Book and Giro currencies are issued by the commercial banks in the form of loans.

These means of payment are in circulation in the economy and among private individuals when payment is made by bank transfer.

States, companies and private individuals do not have accounts with the central bank.

The exchange rate between the central bank currency and the book or Giro currencies is 1:1.

When you withdraw cash, you are essentially exchanging your Giro currency for central bank currency.

Central Bank Currency

Central bank currency is created when the central bank buys debt securities or shares from commercial banks or grants a loan to a commercial bank.

The central bank currency is created out of nothing and is simply a number that is credited to the seller's account. If the seller wants cash, it is printed. In the eurozone, the European Central Bank / ECB is prohibited from buying government bonds directly from the states to prevent direct state financing.

The government bonds are sold by the state to selected banks through an auction.

This is known as the primary market. These financial market participants can then sell the government bonds on to other interested parties such as insurance companies, pension funds, the ECB or even private individuals. This is known as the secondary market.

Depending on the policy currently being pursued, the ECB either buys a few government bonds or almost all of them. Until a few years ago, the ECB bought almost all government bonds on offer and much more. Some economists regard this behavior as covert state financing.

They argue that participants in the capital market have the assurance that the ECB will buy everything.

Another point that is influenced by the central banks is interest rates.

The central banks set the interest rate that banks have to pay when they borrow central bank currency. At the same time, the central bank determines how high the interest rates are when banks store funds at the central bank. Now you should have an idea of what a central bank does.

I am aware that this is only a very superficial view. In the appendix of this book, you will locate sources where you can read about this topic in greater depth.

Book or Giro Currency

The book or Giro currency is issued by commercial banks. It is created when loans are granted.

When a loan is granted, the corresponding credit volume is simply credited to the borrower's account. At this moment, book, or Giro currency is created out of nothing.

However, banks are not allowed to grant loans at will. Each loan must be backed by a percentage of central bank currency. In addition, banks must meet an equity ratio to be able to absorb any loan defaults.

The equity ratio is influenced by the risk involved in granting a loan. A loan for a property is not as risky as a car loan, as the vehicle can be damaged and would therefore have to accept a loss in value or total loss.

We assume an equity ratio of 9%, which makes it easier to do some calculations later and is far higher than the real figures.

The percentage of the deposited central bank currency is between 0% for loans with a term of more than two years and 1% for short-term loans up to a maximum of two years. This brings us, with the equity ratio, to 10%, which the bank must have as reserves.

The bank calculates the interest due on a loan as follows:

In Europe, the EURIBOR is often used as the base interest rate.

In simple terms, the EURIBOR is the interest rate when banks lend money to each other. This is normally in the range of the ECB's key interest rates.

Added to this is the interest that the banks themselves charge. This interest includes a risk component, administrative costs and the profit that the bank wants to make.

We see that fiat currencies are not backed by physical assets such as gold. It is based exclusively on debt.

As a counter-argument, it can be argued that these debts are covered by a good. The loan was used to purchase an item. While this is true, it does not consider that items can break and credit is used for bad investments.

Now that you have a rough overview of currency creation, let's look at two aspects of currencies. Interest rates and inflation.

Interest

In this section, we look at what functions interest actually has, or rather should have.

In doing so, we assume that the amount to be lent is a real available means of payment. The lender has generated a currency surplus by saving and forgoing consumption, and can lend this.

The first function of interest is basically a fee.

The borrower transfers future income into the present. The fee for this transfer is the interest.

I, as a borrower, would like to buy a new washing machine because my old one is broken. Let's say 600.-, I could earn that 600.- in 6 months by saving and not consuming. So, I could buy this washing machine in 6 months. However, my problem is that I need the washing machine now.

So, I have to transfer the 600 that I would have in 6 months to the present. This is made possible by a loan that comes with an interest surcharge.

This surcharge, the interest, can therefore be considered a fee for a service.

Conversely, you can also say that the lender is forgoing consumption today because I have his 600. The consideration for this renunciation of consumption is therefore interest.

A second, essential function of interest is risk assessment.

Here is a small example:

You lend a family member 1000.-. The interest you charge will probably be somewhere between 0% and a pizza at your favorite Italian restaurant. Since you know your family member, you can be pretty sure that you'll get your 1000 back on the agreed date.

But what about a stranger you don't know? You would demand collateral and set a much higher interest rate than for your family member.

We can therefore see that the interest rate enables a risk assessment.

Let's take a look at this risk assessment on a large scale. A state needs new means of payment and issues new government bonds.

If this state is chronically bankrupt and always teetering on the brink, it will have to offer high-interest rates to find buyers for its bonds. If it offers interest rates that are too low, this state will not sell any bonds as the risk is too high for investors.

If the issuing state is wealthy and meets its obligations promptly, it will have to pay less interest on its bonds. The risk for investors is lower.

Now that you know the two main functions of interest rates, let's take a look at what is happening to interest rates today.

The fact that the central bank can change the interest rates for banks as it sees fit and has bought up almost all government bonds unchecked means that the interest rate functions have been overridden.

Some German government bonds were issued with negative interest rates.

This means that investors get back less than they invested.

Central banks use interest rates to control the amount of currency. The higher the central bank interest rates, the more expensive loans become, and the fewer loans are granted. This means that less new book or Giro currency enters circulation.

At the same time, banks will also hold more central bank currency in their accounts and share in the interest profits. Savers will be encouraged to leave their balances in their savings accounts and thus take currency out of circulation.

More on this at the velocity of circulation.

The lower the central bank interest rates are, the more loans are granted. This means that the newly created means of payment are cheap. This puts more currency into circulation. As a result, savers' saving balances also come back into circulation through consumption.

Until the early 2020s, we were operating in a zero-interest rate environment for almost a decade. This meant that interest had completely lost its actual function.

Penalty or negative interest was payable by banks if they parked too much central bank currency at the central bank. They were therefore penalized.

Unfortunately, this shift away from the actual interest rate functions had major side effects and makes an unstable system even more unstable. As a result of the many cheap loans, bubbles have formed on almost all markets.

The cheap means of payment were used to speculate on the stock exchanges and real estate markets. These are two markets out of many.

Assuming you pay 1% interest on a loan and make 5% profit by speculating on the stock market with the loan amount, you have made a good deal.

This cheap money is one of the reasons why prices have risen since 2022 and are still rising.

On the following pages, I will show you some of the bubbles that have built up due to the almost non-existent interest rates.

Zombie Company

The term zombie company crops up in the headlines from time to time.

Very few people know what it means. A zombie company is heavily indebted and cannot service the interest on current loans from its resources. The company is highly unprofitable.

Thanks to the cheap loans, the zombie company is paying off its interest debt with new loans.

Basically, the company would have long since gone bankrupt and disappeared from the market. The cheap loans enable the company to keep itself alive artificially. An undead company or a zombie.

These zombies can be found in almost all industries, including banking and insurance.

Zombies cause two main problems.

Firstly, they tie up resources such as capital, employees, machinery, equipment and real estate. This means that the tied-up resources are not available to healthy companies and therefore hinder the growth of healthy companies.

Secondly, the zombies are a ticking time bomb. If interest rates rise and the zombies can no longer service their debts, the loans will default, which could put the lending bank in serious difficulties. In addition, there will suddenly be large numbers of unemployed people who will no longer be able to meet their obligations due to a lack of income.

Since the ECB raised interest rates, we have seen an increase in company insolvencies. Some of them were zombies.

You might think that because there are so few zombie companies, the issue is manageable. Far from it, the proportion of zombies worldwide is around 30 percent on average. In the energy and consumer durables sectors, such as automobiles, it is around 70% and 45% respectively. (as of 2020). Experts expect the numbers to be just as high in the EU.

As you can see, zombies are not a marginal phenomenon. It affects almost every third company.

Stock Market Bubble

On the stock markets, cheap loans have led to share price increases that are not covered by the real value of the companies.

On the one hand, companies are buying their shares with borrowed cash. These buy-backs reduce the number of shares available on the stock markets. This increases the share price and artificially drives up the value of the company.

If share buybacks are carried out using the company's own capital reserves, this is not normally a problem. This can prevent a takeover of the company by a competitor.

On the other hand, the cheap loans fuel speculation with borrowed cash.

With a loan interest rate of 1% and a speculative profit of 5%, 4% remains as profit.

However, this behavior also leads to share prices that have nothing to do with the real value of the issuing company.

You may now understand how it can be that despite the real economic slump of 2020 and 2021, the German share index (DAX) has risen by around 17%.

From 13385 points on 2.1.2020 to 16152 points on 4.1.2022

This price increase contrasts with economic output of minus 3.8% in 2020 and plus 3.6% in 2021 in relation to the respective previous year.

This results in growth of minus 0.2% in relation to 2019.

As you can see, the share price gains of the 40 DAX companies have little to do with economic performance.

Real Estate Bubble

Similar scenes are playing out in the real estate market.

After neither government bonds nor conventional savings accounts had yielded interest profits, these assets increasingly flowed into real estate. Real estate replaced government bonds and fixed-interest securities as a safe investment product, as it was no longer possible to realize interest profits with these securities.

Here, too, the simple rules of supply and demand apply.

The higher the demand for a small supply, the higher the prices. There is also speculation in the real estate market with a lot of borrowed money and a further shortage of supply.

Ultimately, this leads to higher rents and fewer and fewer people being able to afford an apartment, let alone their own home.

After the ECB raised interest rates sharply again in 2023, we are seeing more and more building contractors and real estate companies having to file for bankruptcy. The interest rate hikes have made construction even more expensive (in addition to the increased cost of materials) and more and more property developers can no longer afford this interest burden, if at all.

As a result, fewer homes are being built and the situation for the poorer sections of the population is getting worse.

Other factors also play an important role in the rise in property prices. However, these are more likely to be attributed to incompetent politicians and will not be discussed further here.

However, at the end of the book, I will show you some sources that illustrate the political failure.

On the following pages, I will show you what consequences these currency expansions can have for purchasing power. Everyone is now feeling the consequences. In October 2022, inflation was 10.6% on average in the EU. In 2023, inflation slowly fell again following the interest rate hikes.

Inflation

Inflation has recently been equated with the increase in the price of goods.

In my opinion, this definition is indifferent. Inflation in the literal sense is only the expansion of the currency supply. The rise in consumer prices can be a consequence of inflation.

These price increases can occur at different levels and at different times in different markets.

Consumer prices are shown using the consumer price index. A virtual basket of goods is used for measurement. In Germany, the basket contains around 700 goods and services that a private household in Germany consumes.

The goods are weighted differently, meaning that baked goods are treated differently to rent.

However, this index has a few problems.

The first is that goods can be exchanged at any time. If, for example, a 300-gram fillet of beef is replaced by a sausage, this has a massive impact on the meat price that is measured.

The same happens if the weighting of individual products or product groups is changed.

For example, the housing sector in Germany was reduced from 32.5% to 26% in 2023.

Another issue is that not all citizens are affected equally. The following example illustrates this:

Person A lives in a city and also works there. Person A is a vegetarian and only travels by public transport or bicycle. Person A will hardly be directly influenced by price increases for meat products or fuel.

Person B lives on the countryside and works in the city. Person A has a balanced diet and is dependent on a car. Person B will feel a price increase in meat products and fuel much more strongly.

I hope you can see where I'm going with this.

The index gives too inaccurate a picture of the average inflation rate. If we were to compare the overall economic performance with the increase in the amount of currency, we would have a much broader and balanced picture.

If economic output increases in relation to the currency supply, the individual euro is worth more, which increases purchasing power and prosperity.

If the economy grows at the same rate as the money supply, nothing changes. Purchasing power is the same and prices do not change either. Your prosperity therefore remains constant.

If the amount of currency increases more than the economic output, we speak of inflation. This means that the currency loses purchasing power, your prosperity decreases and prices rise.

As you can see, interest rates and currency supply extensions, as well as the resulting inflation, are closely intertwined.

By comparing the economic strength and the amount of currency, you can depict inflation much more broadly and smooth out the differences between person A and person B from the example.

Velocity

Another factor that should not be neglected is the velocity of circulation.

It shows how much is consumed with a single unit of currency.

To illustrate this, let me give you a small example:

You go to the canteen and eat your lunch with a drink. You pay with a 10.- bill. The canteen owner takes this 10.- bill and allows himself two after-work beers in his favorite pub. The cost is 10.- The Pup-owner takes this 10 and uses it to pay for the cab ride after work. The cab driver uses the 10 received from the pup-owner to refuel.

We see that these 10.- have paid for goods and services worth 40.-. The more goods and services are paid for with the 10.-, the higher the velocity of circulation. The lower the velocity of circulation, the more is saved.

Saving takes these 10.- out of circulation and thus prevents them from circulating. As I mentioned above, price rises can have different causes and do not occur simultaneously in all markets.

Supply and Demand

Another reason for an increase in prices is supply and demand.

If a lot of demand meets little supply, prices will rise. The same applies when a lot of currency meets little supply.

As a result, consumption was rather restrained in 2020, as nobody knew exactly what would happen next. So, people saved and thus reduced the rate of circulation.

When stores reopened and the situation eased, people spent their savings again, thereby increasing the velocity of circulation. As a result, a lot of currency met a limited supply and prices rose.

In conclusion, we can say that the manipulation of interest rates and currencies is the reason for many grievances.

Unfortunately, these grievances generally affect the poorer sections of the population, who are actually the least responsible.

Long-standing problems such as pensions, healthcare systems and poverty are largely due to these manipulations and cannot be solved with this system.

Misconception

In 2022, the inflation rate in the EU was 10.6%.

This means that prices rose by 10.6% compared to 2021.

In 2023, the inflation rate was around 6.5% compared to 2022.

This means that the inflation rate compared to 2021 is 17%.

Prices are not falling; they are just rising more slowly!

Only if we had negative inflation rates would prices fall.

I hope I have been able to give you an understanding of the basic functions and effects of the fiat currency system. If I was successful, you will understand Web3 much better and recognize the benefits more easily.

Web3

As I mentioned in the introduction, Web3 also involves the transfer of values and the associated verification of ownership claims to these values.

Put simply, in Web3, it is possible to clearly prove who owns a value. The underlying technology is called DLT. Distributed Ledger Technology. In slightly less cumbersome terms, this involves identical copies of the same cash book that are stored on many computers.

It is therefore immediately noticeable if one copy has been manipulated, as it no longer matches the other copies.

A blockchain and a DAG, Directed Acyclic Graph, are two ways of achieving this goal.

DLT therefore describes the superordinate technology, and a blockchain or a DAG are the subordinate options for implementation.

On the following pages, you will learn how a blockchain works and how it solves the task. You will then see how a DAG works in principle and how it arrives at a suitable solution.

The Blockchain

Basically, a blockchain is a cash book and with each new block, another page is added to the cash book in chronological order.

I would like to use the following example to illustrate the concept and give you an understanding of how it works:

An Analog Form

Let's take a community of ten people who meet daily at 17:00 to complete their transactions.

Everyone who has purchased services or goods from a member pays for them in the presence of all community members. This ensures that every member has the same level of knowledge and at the same time the payment is verified by all members.

There is a consensus regarding transactions and everyone knows how much money they have, as everyone is aware of their income and expenditure.

Now we expand our community to 1000 members.

Since the number of transactions is now increasing and the living space has expanded, the meetings no longer make sense.

Now all transactions between members are written on a piece of paper. This receipt contains the names of the parties involved, the price paid, the goods, the exact time and, of course, both signatures of the parties involved.

This receipt is then placed in a kind of mailbox. Once a day, this mailbox is emptied by a member, it doesn't always have to be the same person, whoever has the time and inclination empties the mailbox.

The receipts are checked by this person and written in chronological order on a proper sheet of paper. The sheet is given a consecutive page number so that it can be filed in the correct place.

Once the fair copy has been completed, 999 copies are made and distributed to the members. The members check the final copy and, if there are no obvious errors, place it at the back of the existing final copies.

This means that every member has the same level of knowledge and everyone knows how much money they have. Of course, you would now have to check and calculate who has paid how much to whom based on the final records, but it is possible as all transactions are available in chronological order for each member.

Provided there are no complaints, there is once again consensus in the community.

The examples shown above illustrate the concept of a blockchain. On a blockchain, all transactions can be viewed by anyone at any time.

This means that anyone can see how many means of payment someone has.

This makes a blockchain by far the most transparent way of documenting transactions.

On the following pages, I will show you how this concept has been digitized and is used worldwide. We thus increase the theoretical number of members to eight billion and expand the living space to the entire earth.

The Real Blockchain

First, we need to digitize our analogue participants and tools.

I am basing this on the Bitcoin blockchain:

Nodes:

These replace the members who physically store the cash book. The digital copies of the entire blockchain are stored on the nodes.

Miner:

The miners are the computers that create the final version and check the final versions of other miners.

Mem Pool/ Mailbox:

The mem pool, memory pool is where the receipts are collected, which are later written into plain text by the miners.

Wallet / members:

Anyone can participate in the network with a wallet and thus represents a member. The balance is stored in the wallet and is also used to carry out transactions with other wallets.

All these participants are connected to each other via the Internet.

Anyone who has access to the Internet can participate in the network on an equal footing.

I will now explain the functions of the four participants in more detail.

Wallets:

On a blockchain, all transactions take place peer-to-peer, from participant to participant, comparable to cash payments in real life.

As we do not necessarily know our counterpart, it is important that we can carry out transactions without having to trust our counterpart. As there is no external party acting as a controlling body in these transactions, we need another option that is not based on trust in our counterpart.

Asymmetric encryption is used for this purpose.

This consists of a key pair consisting of the public key and the private key. The public key is comparable to your bank account number. Anyone who knows your account number can transfer funds to you. In addition, the public key can be used to read messages that have been encrypted with the private key.

The private key can be compared with your bank account access data. You can use the private key to initiate transactions. You can also use the private key to encrypt messages that can only be read with the corresponding public key.

You can quickly derive a public key from the private key, but the reverse is not possible.

Here is an example to illustrate this:

You have a raw egg. This egg is your private key. To generate a public key from it, drop the egg on the floor. The result of this mess is your public key. You will not be able to reassemble a whole raw egg from this mess and thus deduce the private key.

Transactions:

Now let's take a look at how a transaction works.

You send a Bitcoin to a wallet. To achieve this, enter the recipient's public key and confirm the transaction with your private key.

Now this one Bitcoin is sent to the other wallet.

At the same time, a message about the amount sent is encrypted with your private key and sent to the recipient by separate post. The recipient can now read the encrypted message with your public key, which they know because they can see which wallet the Bitcoin was sent from.

If this message says: "One Bitcoin", the recipient knows that the transaction has not been manipulated and is correct.

This transaction is now transferred to the mem pool with a timestamp. The fact that you have triggered the transaction with your private key means that the "receipt" is signed by you. The receipt of the transaction on the recipient wallet serves as the recipient's signature.

This method eliminates the need for an external control instance for the transaction.

Mem Pool:

All signed and time-stamped "receipts" end up in the mem pool.

If a new block is not verified by the other network participants, all transactions contained in the block also fall back into the mem pool.

There are several possibilities why this happens, but they are not essential for understanding.

The Miner:

A new block is created in the Bitcoin network approximately every ten minutes.

A clean copy is created. All miners are in competition with each other, and everyone tries to create the fair copy as quickly as possible. When a miner has finished the block, all other miners switch over and check the block for correctness.

Once the fair copy or block has been checked, and no errors have been found, the miner who created the block receives a reward in the form of Bitcoin.

This is the only way Bitcoins are created. They are always a reward for the miner's work. The reward, the block reward, halves after 210,000 blocks, which takes around 4 years.

The reward started at 50 BTC and will have already been reduced to 3.125 BTC by around April 24.

The last BTC is expected in 2140.

Nodes:

Once the new block has been confirmed, a copy is appended to the end of the blocks that have already been saved.

This creates a chain of blocks. The newest block is the last one. The blockchain.

The ten-minute cycle is used to synchronize the nodes. As the nodes are distributed all over the world, they do not receive the new blocks at the same time. After ten minutes, the nodes are back at the same level of knowledge and therefore synchronized.

Satoshi Nakamoto

With the introduction of the Bitcoin blockchain in 2009 by Satoshi Nakamoto, all the processes described above were published.

However, this does not mean that Satoshi Nakamoto invented all these concepts. Nakamoto rearranged existing concepts and developments and thereby achieved that a blockchain works the way it does today.

This is in no way intended to diminish Nakamoto's outstanding achievement, it is just important to know that he was able to draw on existing concepts.

A brief historical review

Ralph Merkle:

1974 Discovery of asymmetric encryption

Rivest, Shamir and Adleman:

1977 First public key encryption method

Diffie, Hellman and Merkle:

1978 Diffie-Hellman key exchange

Ralph Merkle:

1979 Merkle tree with hash function

Merkle and Damgård:

1979 MD hash function

Stornetta and Haber:

1991 Blockchain function

NIST and NSA:

1993 Publication of the Secure Hash Algorithm

Nick Szabo:

1996 Smart Contracts

Precursor of Bitcoin

David Chaum:

1983 E-Cash

Nick Szabo:

1999 Bit-Gold

We can see that the main components of the Bitcoin blockchain date back to the seventies of the previous century.

However, it was the new combination of elements by Nakamoto that made a digital peer-to-peer cash system possible that we know today as Bitcoin.

D.A.G./ Directed Acyclic Graph

A DAG is another way of building a decentralized network.

The result is the same as with a blockchain, only the way to get there is significantly different.

I will explain the process below so that you understand the concept.

In a DAG, transactions are not stored in blocks and then appended to the end of the blockchain. It is basically a constant flow of information that is stored. In a DAG, many transactions are processed and confirmed in parallel.

The results are then forwarded to the computers in a "gossip over gossip" process, which store the results chronologically.

You can imagine it like this:

Max tells Monika that he has just watched Jim pay at the supermarket checkout, and Monika updates Max that Veronika has just paid at the fashion store. Monika tells her friend Sandra that Max told her how he saw Jim pay at the supermarket checkout and how she herself saw Veronika pay at the fashion store ...

This chatting leads to the constant flow of information mentioned at the beginning.

In a DAG, the information is not written in plain text and then attached to the existing cash book. As soon as the information arrives at the nodes, it is stored chronologically.

This works because the transactions have already been verified and do not require any subsequent checks when they are rewritten or blocks are created.

To make a transaction, I have to confirm two transactions beforehand. As a reward for the two confirmed transactions, there are virtually no transaction fees for my transaction.

This accelerates the network with every transaction. The more transactions, the more transactions have to be confirmed in advance and the faster the network becomes.

With this system, several transactions can be processed in parallel and all network participants can be informed simultaneously.

With this technology, DAGs can process an almost infinite number of transactions per second, depending of course, on the number of network participants.

The more participants, the more transactions.

MIOTA and HEDERA Hashgraph use this technology and can process around 100,000 transactions per second.

Challenges

I hope I have been able to introduce you to two different possibilities of a decentralized network on the previous pages.

In this chapter, I would like to show you the trilemma of DLT applications, especially blockchain.

I will also show you two possible solutions for how Web3 responds to the various challenges.

As with any technology, there is light and shade, and Web3 is no different. I am only referring here to the technical challenges.

Trilemma

Blockchain technology operates in three areas of tension.

The speed at which transactions can be processed. The degree of decentralization and the degree of security in the network. The chart shows that it is not possible to fulfill all three fields' 100 percent.

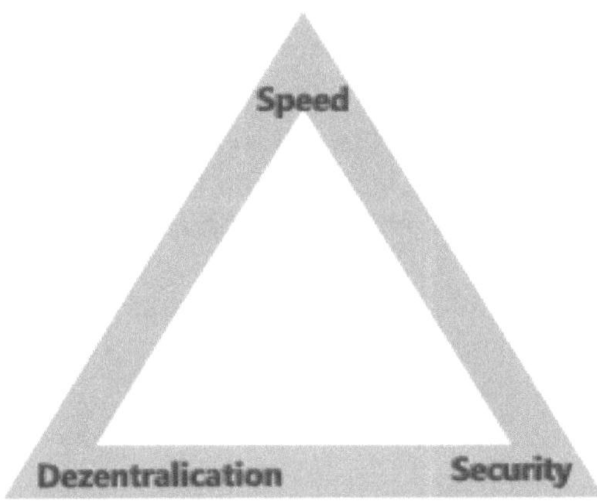

The faster a network is, the less secure and more centralized it becomes.

The more secure it is, the slower and more centralized it becomes.

The more decentralized the network is, the slower and less secure it becomes.

This is one of the reasons why there are so many cryptocurrencies. This is due to the focus of the individual applications and which of the three fields is preferred.

Bitcoin manages around seven transactions per second (TPS), Dash manages 48 TPS and, for comparison, VISA is around 24,000 TPS.

Bitcoin is very secure and as decentralized as possible, which means that its speed suffers. Dash, on the other hand, makes sacrifices in terms of decentralization and security, thereby gaining speed.

As you can see, on the technical side, there are some fundamental decisions that need to be made before a decentralized network is developed.

There are already many applications that solve the problem of speed and bring Bitcoin, for example, to well over 100,000 TPS.

Second Layer

L2 or second layer are used for this purpose.

These are networks that build on an existing one. In the case of Bitcoin, for example, a second layer is called the Lightning Network.

In the Lightning Network, transactions are not processed directly on the Bitcoin blockchain. The concept behind this is simple. The amount to be transferred is transferred to the Lightning network and then sent to the recipient. So-called payment channels are used.

As soon as the payment has been made, the channel can be closed again.

Basically, you have your wallet on the Lightning network, with which you can send and receive payments.

The number of payment channels available depends on the number of computers participating in the Lightning network. In May 2022, 84,000 channels were available and 34,000 computers/nodes were participating in the network.

Basically, the transactions are bundled on the Lightning Network. Let's assume that 1000 different transactions are carried out on the Lightning Network. The total value of all transactions amounts to two bitcoins. The total volume is now stored and verified on the Bitcoin blockchain, not all individual transactions.

Thus, 1000 transactions on the Lightning Network became one transaction on the Bitcoin network. By saving the results after the transactions on the Bitcoin blockchain, security, and decentralization are maintained.

Similar second layer applications also exist for the Ethereum blockchain. Polygon, Optimism, Arbitrum and IMX are among the best known.

The developers and respective community members work daily on solutions to master the known challenges. There are new suggestions and solutions for a wide variety of challenges on an almost daily basis, and there is no end to development in sight.

In this short chapter, I have tried to give you an understanding of the advantages and disadvantages of the new technology.

You have also learned that development is far from complete.

The question arises: "How can all this happen in such a short time?"

Developments that used to take years and horrendous sums of money often only need a few months to be implemented.

Open Source

Most of you will have heard of the LINUX operating system.

Linus Torvalds began developing his own operating system in the early 1990s. He made his development freely available to other programmers. They began to develop the system further and developed programs that ran on this operating system.

They also made these new developments freely available and could be adopted, adapted or modified by other programmers.

Today, you can still install a Linux operating system on your computer free of charge and download the one that suits you best from a wide range of applications.

The font used in this book, Ubuntu, is also open source and may be used freely.

However, the success story lies less in the operating systems for computers than in the control of countless devices and machines.

A modern elevator runs on Linux. Your car is controlled by Linux. Smartphone, Linux. Blu-ray player, Linux. The list could go on for pages.

The Advantage

You don't have to develop every software application from scratch.

You take existing software and adapt it to your requirements. You make your new development available to others, who may use or adapt it for a different application. This saves time and money, and everyone benefits from the new developments.

Another advantage is the security of the various applications. As all applications are freely visible, any programming errors are detected and rectified much more quickly.

Every time an existing application is built upon, the developer of the new application will check the security of the application they are using for errors and change it if necessary.

This is precisely how many applications work on the web3. You can download the program code of the Bitcoin blockchain at any time and use it to create your own cryptocurrency.

In the NFT area, more on this later, NFT communities make their developments available to other NFT projects. This saves new projects from having to develop their own programs.

In return, the new projects provide NFTs for the helping community.

By sharing software developments worldwide, it is possible for new applications to become available in a much shorter time and for the development curve to rise steeply.

In a world where everyone cooks their own soup and doesn't let anyone look at their cards, this kind of development is not possible.

This is a crucial point in Web3, it's all about collaboration.

Applications

On the following pages, I would like to show you which applications exist.

The applications range from cryptocurrencies, decentralized financial instruments and decentralized identities to non-fungible tokens.

I aim to give you an overview of how the new applications work and how they differ from existing Web 2.0 applications.

You will realize that many models that we have taken for granted up to now are being turned completely upside down.

This will create countless opportunities to develop business models that are at times far superior to today's models.

I hope you enjoy discovering these applications.

Cryptocurrencies

On Coingecko, a website that shows the current prices of cryptocurrencies, 11214 different cryptocurrencies are listed. (As of Dec. 2, 2023)

However, the term cryptocurrency is not appropriate for most cryptocurrencies. Roughly speaking, these crypto assets can be divided into four categories:

Cryptocurrencies

These are crypto assets that are designed as pure currencies.

These include Bitcoin (BTC), Litecoin (LTC) and Monero (XMR). Stable coins also fall into this category.

Stablecoins are based on the US dollar, among other things. The exchange rate of these stablecoins is always one US dollar, plus/minus a few cents.

These include the US dollar Tether (USDT), the US dollar Coin (USDC) and the DAI, to name but a few.

There are also stablecoins that represent the euro or gold, for example.

Utility Token

A utility token is best compared to a voucher.

You can use this voucher to make use of applications or services in the respective ecosystem.

Another option is to maintain the underlying infrastructure, for example. A utility token is used to pay for services such as transactions, smart contracts (more on this later) and much more. Ethereum (ETH), Solana (SOL) and Tron (TRX) serve as examples.

Security Token

A security token is comparable to a bond or participation certificate.

With a bond, you provide liquidity to a company or a state without acquiring a claim to ownership of the company or the state.

You can be relatively certain that you will get your invested liquidity back at the end of the term with an interest premium.

With a profit participation certificate, you participate in the profits of the company without having any ownership rights. These include Polymath (POLY) and Tezos (XTZ), among many others.

Equity or Capital Token

Equity tokens are digitized shares in companies. These are traded on various exchanges.

Bitcoin

Cryptocurrencies in particular, such as Bitcoin, offer an alternative to the existing fiat currency system.

The maximum number of Bitcoins is mathematically limited to just under 21 million. This number will be reached approximately in the year 2140. This means that Bitcoin cannot be manipulated at will. It is not possible to increase the number at will or intervene in the protocol in any other way.

In addition, Bitcoin does not require an external authority to verify transfers. Bitcoin can be used across countries, the fees on the Lightning Network are negligible and transactions are completed in just a few minutes.

Anyone who has ever made a payment to a non-SEPA country knows what I'm talking about.

With Bitcoin, you don't have to trust any external authority, such as the bank, that the initiated transfer will actually be triggered.

At the same time, all transactions are stored transparently and can be viewed at any time.

Bitcoin and the Rest

Bitcoin has an important unique selling point compared to all other cryptocurrencies.

Bitcoin belongs to no one and therefore to everyone.

The Bitcoin network was handed over to the general public by Satoshi Nakamoto.

There is neither a Bitcoin Ltd. nor a foundation that looks after Bitcoin.

The developers who work on Bitcoin do so voluntarily and are not employed by Bitcoin.

The situation is different for all other crypto assets. These are backed by companies or foundations. For example, the Ethereum Foundation or Circle behind the USDC.

Settlement

Another advantage lies in the settlement, the final booking of transactions.

In the banking system, transactions between banks are not finally settled daily. The account holder at bank A receives a payment from the account holder at bank B. This means that bank B owes bank A the amount of the payment.

As many such transactions take place every day and other banks are involved, these payments are offset and finally settled once a week, month, or quarter.

If Bank B still owes Bank A something after the final settlement, this amount is transferred to Bank A.

This procedure is practical and reduces transactions, but is also associated with a risk. If Bank B gets into payment difficulties, it damages Bank A. This can lead to a chain reaction and cause many banks to fail.

With Cryptocurrencies, settlement takes place with every new block. The transactions are finally settled and booked.

Bank Access

Another problem that cryptocurrencies could solve is the fact that, according to the World Bank, around 24 percent of the world's population does not have access to a bank account.

There are various reasons for this. Too little money to open an account, no bank nearby, bank fees too high, no way to prove identity and a few other reasons.

With the constant expansion of internet access and cryptocurrencies, new opportunities are opening up for these people to generate an income. They are becoming their own bank, so to speak. A wallet on your smartphone is all you need to make and receive payments. There are no bank fees and the transaction costs are usually manageable.

This gives these people the opportunity to set up their own small business and participate in the market.

You can therefore see that cryptocurrency could contribute to the inclusion of almost a quarter of the world's population.

Tamper-proof

Now, I would like to put Bitcoin in relation to today's fiat currency system.

You know that there will be just under 21 million Bitcoins around the year 2140. This means that inflation is not a problem with Bitcoin.

The quantity cannot be changed. This means that we have eliminated the part of rising prices that is based on inflation.

Since interest rates can hardly be manipulated either — there is no central bank — the free-market sets interest rates. This means that the interest rate can reflect the information inherent in it.

These are risk and the service fee for transferring future values to the present.

This means that price fluctuations are only driven by supply and demand.

The more people understand this and use Bitcoin as an alternative currency, the less price fluctuations will occur.

This will ensure that Bitcoin becomes a store of value and thus real money.

Once Bitcoin has achieved its function as a store of value, numerous difficulties can be solved.

Pensions

I would like to mention pensions as an example.

Today, people who are working pay the pensions of people who have retired. There is talk of an intergenerational contract, even though no one has signed it.

The problem is, that there are more and more older people and therefore pensioners who have to be financed by fewer and fewer young, working people.

In addition, a currency that loses two percent of its purchasing power every year or even 10%, as we saw in 2022, is used for this purpose.

We are now assuming that Bitcoin will establish itself as a store of value and will therefore not lose two percent of its purchasing power each year by design. It would therefore be possible for the system to be converted.

Every working person now saves for themselves, which would solve the demographic problem in the long term. Of course, a transitional solution is needed for today's pensioners. If we take into account non-manipulated interest rates, this could be one way to achieve this transition.

At the end of July 2022, the inflation rate was just under eight percent in the eurozone. Let's assume that the European Central Bank (ECB) raises key interest rates to three percent. This means that we still have negative real interest rates in terms of purchasing power. Namely, minus five percent real interest.

This means that the loss of purchasing power has been reduced over time, but not stopped and certainly not turned into a positive trend.

If Bitcoin establishes itself as a store of value and interest rates develop on the free market, we will automatically have positive real interest rates, as the problem of inflation will no longer exist.

This would enable pension funds to realize real profits again.

This system also works in a one hundred percent gold standard, in which the means of payment in circulation are 100% backed by gold.

This brief excursion is intended to show you the difference between a fiat currency such as the Euro and Bitcoin or a gold standard.

Smart-Contract

A smart contract is basically nothing more than an "if/then" logic.

If a previously defined event occurs, a previously defined action is triggered.

For example:

When an Ether is deposited, an image is sent back to this address.

Some readers may wonder what's so great about this? The smart contract only consists of two states, the "if" and the "then".

If we look at digitalization, it also only consists of two states, "1" and "0", and we see what can be done with it every day. It's the same with smart contracts. By linking several if/then logics, complex processes can be automated.

As these smart contracts are stored on the blockchain, they cannot be manipulated and can be viewed at any time. This makes it possible to execute complex processes automatically without a control instance.

The risk with smart contracts lies in their programming. Regardless of which processes are to be automated, if the smart contract has an error, large amounts of crypto assets may no longer be accessible. It happens time and again that no payout is defined for a smart contract.

To explain this, you buy a digital asset. To achieve this, you transfer 0.1 Ether to a smart contract. As soon as this 0.1 ether arrives in the smart contract, the smart contract will in turn send the digital value to your wallet.

As we can see, all payment processes for digital assets and goods run via smart contracts. The purchase price is always transferred to a smart contract, which then triggers an action. This also means that the seller must have the purchase price transferred from the smart contract to their wallet to be able to use the proceeds.

If the smart contract is programmed incorrectly, this transaction option will not be available.

Cryptocurrencies are always push transactions.

The holder of the cryptocurrencies must initiate a transaction, always. As only the holder has the private keys to sign the transaction.

The same applies to a smart contract. In this case, the smart contract is the owner, and only it can initiate a transaction. If the payout has not been activated during programming, the payments remain in the smart contract and cannot be accessed.

Many millions of US dollars have already been lost due to incorrectly programmed smart contracts.

But they are not lost, you can view them on the blockchain, you just don't have access to them.

Smart contracts are an extension of the possibilities of a blockchain.

However, this requires blockchains that can process smart contracts. The best known are probably Ethereum, Solana, Tron, Avalanche, Cardano, Terra, Polkadot and Binance.

There are many more blockchains and DAGs that can process smart contracts; these are the largest by market capitalization.

E.R.C. Standard

ERC stands for, Ethereum Request for Comment. These standards define how the smart contracts in question are to be programmed.

Basically, the technical documentation. The most commonly used smart contract standards on the Ethereum Chain are the following:

ERC 20:

These smart contracts are used for fungible assets. These include all crypto coins, such as the USDC on the Ethereum blockchain.

ERC 721:

Almost all NFTs are created with this smart contract.

ERC 1155:

You can consider this standard to be a container in which you can store different assets. This can be an NFT and several coins. If you destroy the NFT, you have access to the coins again.

ERC 4337:

This standard enables account abstraction and thus smart wallets.

ERC: 6551:

Token bound account. This links a separate wallet to an ERC 721 NFT.

All these ERC standards originate from an EIP. EIP stands for Ethereum Improvement Proposal.

Developers make proposals to improve the Ethereum network. If the proposals are accepted, they are converted into ERC standards. The number is consecutive.

E.V.M.

Ethereum virtual machine refers to the application within the Ethereum network on which smart contracts are processed.

This EVM can also be used by other blockchain networks. This means that these other networks are compatible with Ethereum and crypto values can be transferred to another blockchain via the so-called bridges.

The best-known EVM networks include

BSC[1] / Binance Smart Chain

Arbitrum[2]

Polygon[3]

Avalanche[4]

Optimism[5]

Fantom[6]

Cronos[7]

Klaytn[8]

---

1. https://thirdweb.com/binance?ref=blog.thirdweb.com

2. https://thirdweb.com/arbitrum?ref=blog.thirdweb.com

3. https://thirdweb.com/polygon?ref=blog.thirdweb.com

4. https://thirdweb.com/avalanche?ref=blog.thirdweb.com

5. https://thirdweb.com/optimism?ref=blog.thirdweb.com

6. https://thirdweb.com/fantom?ref=blog.thirdweb.com

7. https://thirdweb.com/cronos-beta?ref=blog.thirdweb.com

8. https://thirdweb.com/klaytn-cypress?ref=blog.thirdweb.com

Canto[9]

Since these networks use the same Smart Contact standard, the same number is also specified. ERC 20 becomes BEP 20 on the Binance Smart Chain. BEP 20 is also the basis for fungible crypto coins, only on the Binance Smart Chain.

9. https://thirdweb.com/canto?ref=blog.thirdweb.com

Decentralized Finance

DeFi refers to all applications related to finance.

Decentralized financial services are slowly replacing the banking business as we know it today. This includes lending, investment products, passive income and much more.

But not all DeFi is the same. There are applications where you interact directly with a smart contract on a blockchain and applications that are provided by a company.

I will not differentiate between the two in the rest of this article, as this only adds to the confusion.

It is becoming increasingly difficult for ordinary people to invest their money profitably. Interest on savings or bonds, the safe asset classes, was non-existent until recently. Even if you manage to earn 3% interest, inflation will eat up your profits. 3% interest income and 6% inflation mean you lose 3% per year in real terms.

In short, safe investments and savings products will reduce your wealth over time. This also means that you need to invest in riskier products. Stocks, ETFs, and funds are a good choice.

I showed you at the beginning that there are some lurking risks, as some shares are vastly overvalued and around 30% of companies are considered zombie companies. Finding the right product or security in this environment is almost impossible for the average person.

You would have to invest a lot of time and effort to find the right products for you. As mentioned above, you would have to make a profit of at least 7% to avoid losing wealth.

With rising inflation, profits should also be higher, as otherwise you will lose purchasing power in real terms.

Now that the ECB has raised interest rates again and the banks are passing them on, the situation has eased somewhat. But what alternatives does DeFi offer?

Lending

With lending, you lend your crypto assets.

This can be for a few days or for longer periods. You generate interest income of between 3% and 8% per year.

Interest rates vary as they are recalculated weekly and depend on the cryptocurrency you lend.

Lending is a Lombard loan. This means that the borrower must deposit at least 100% as collateral. The procedure is comparable to a pawnbroker. If you pawn your car, you will not receive the current value of your vehicle in euros, instead is probably only around 60%.

You may be wondering what the point of this is?

Such lending's are used for short-term capital to be liquid.

Suppose a customer's invoice was paid too late, but you have to pay salaries and therefore need short-term liquidity. To avoid having to sell your crypto assets, you borrow against them.

This comes with the advantage that you still benefit from price fluctuations in your crypto assets, as you do not have to sell them. The interest income for this Lombard loan is divided among the "lenders".

Another reason for a Lombard loan is leverage positions.

This involves betting on rising prices and making a profit. To increase profits, you borrow against your crypto assets and buy more crypto assets with the borrowed funds. This increases the number of crypto assets held.

Before the loan period expires, the crypto assets purchased on credit are sold again and the loan is repaid. As the loan is paid out and repaid in US dollars, for example, an additional profit remains after repayment.

This means that price gains were achieved with your own crypto assets and also with those financed via the loan.

Assuming you had to guarantee 100% coverage, you almost doubled your profit in US dollars and thus worked with a double leverage.

- Own crypto assets: 10 coins at $100.- = $1000.-
- Loan 100% covered: $1000.- = 10 coins
- Portfolio value: 20 coins at $100.- = $2000.- Increase in value 50%: 20 coins at $150.- = $3000.-
- Repayment of loan: -$1000.- = $2000.-

Remainder

Without the loan, you would have made a profit of $500.- with your own crypto assets.

With the loan, the profit has increased to $1000.

In reality, it is slightly less, as the interest on the loan was not taken into account in this example.

These were two examples of what Lombard loans and lending are used for. As the loans are at least 100% collateralized, lending is a safe way to generate profits.

However, there are also downsides that you need to be aware of.

While your crypto assets are lended, you have no access to them. If prices fall, you cannot get out until the loan has been repaid. However, you benefit from price gains and thus achieve a kind of compound interest effect.

Let's assume you lend one Bitcoin at 10% interest. As soon as the loan is repaid, you own 1.1 Bitcoin. You now have the opportunity to lend 1.1 Bitcoin, which means a profit of 0.11 Bitcoin at the same interest rate.

I hope I have been able to give you an understanding of the principle of lending, with its advantages and disadvantages. Now let's take a look at another way in which you can generate profits.

Staking

Staking means that you provide cryptocurrencies as collateral.

Let me say a few words about the different consensus mechanisms of blockchains.

The Bitcoin blockchain uses the proof of work consensus mechanism. This means that when a new block, i.e., a clean copy, is created, the creator must invest computing power and therefore energy to create the clean copy. The cost of the energy invested therefore guarantees that the miner works honestly and accurately. If he does not do this and the block is not confirmed by the other network participants, he has spent the energy in vain and loses money.

Another option is the proof of stake consensus mechanism.

A master node operator, as the miners in a proof of stake consensus mechanism are called, must deposit a minimum amount of the respective cryptocurrency as collateral. If the block or the clean copy is not correct and is not confirmed by the other network participants, it loses part of its deposited security and therefore money.

With staking, you provide a master node operator with capital as collateral and in return receive a share of the block rewards. Depending on the blockchain and master node operator, you can earn between around 5% and 30% per year.

The profit depends on the number of master nodes. The fewer master nodes, the higher the profit. Of course, there are disadvantages here too.

While your cryptocurrencies are staked, you have no access to them. If the master node operator performs poorly, your stake may be reduced and you may lose money. This is because you are guaranteeing the correct work of the master node operator with your stake.

With higher profits and therefore fewer master nodes, you are interacting with a little-used blockchain. The less a blockchain is used, the higher the risk. After lending, staking is the second-safest way to earn money.

However, you must make sure that you place your stake with an established and clean master node operator. Ideally, you should spread your investment across several master nodes to spread the risk.

Another option that is very similar to staking relates to Proof of Work blockchains.

Mining

As you already know, the consensus mechanism for Proof of Work blockchains is based on computing power and the resulting energy requirements.

You can join a cloud miner. Cloud miners operate computers to create blocks on a PoW blockchain. You can rent mining computers with your deposit.

Depending on the blockchain and miner, double-digit profits are possible in relation to the crypto assets you have deposited.

If the prices of the crypto assets you have deposited fall, you will make a loss in relation to the US dollar. The same applies to staking, of course.

As you can see, this is another way to generate passive income. As with all the options shown so far, you do not have access to your cryptocurrencies as long as you are invested.

The price risk also remains in this case.

With this type of investment, it is important that the miner use up-to-date Mining-Machines.

Please note that the possible profits can fluctuate greatly. Depending on the price of electricity, the level of difficulty and the value of the cryptocurrency.

If the price of the chosen cryptocurrency falls, it can happen that the income no longer covers the operating expenses, and you make losses.

Unfortunately, there are many scammers in this field who basically use a pyramid scheme.

The higher the promise of profit, the higher the probability that it is a scam. I am not invested in cloud mining myself.

Liquidity Mining and Arbitrage

Liquidity mining is a procedure that does not occur in traditional banking and exchange systems.

The first three options shown are also used in a similar form in the traditional environment.

However, this is where decentralized exchanges, or DEX for short, come into play.

I need to go into some detail here to explain how they work. It may well be that this is a little unwieldy to understand at first.

However, you must understand the function so that you can get an idea of it.

Let's start with a centralized exchange, as they are used today.

A centralized exchange has an order book. This book lists the buyers and sellers of a share, for example. In other words, someone wants to sell a share for X amount.

On the other side is a buyer who would like to buy a share at price Y. If the seller cannot sell his share, he will lower the price until he finds a buyer.

The last sale indicates the price of the share.

On the buyer's side, it can happen that he cannot find a seller for his offered price Y. He will therefore raise his offered purchase price until a seller accepts the offer.

The order book is visible to everyone, so everyone can decide for themselves whether they want to buy or sell.

Basically, the system is based on supply and demand. If the new selling price is higher than the last selling price, the share price has risen. If the price falls, the share price has fallen.

The same applies to currency transactions on central exchanges. In each case, there is always a buyer and a seller. This means that there is always liquidity, as the buyer pays the seller on agreement.

Decentralized exchanges do not have an order book.

This means that buyers and sellers are not necessarily face to face.

You therefore need an entirely different way to process these transactions and determine a price. In addition, the DEX must also provide liquidity, as a buyer does not necessarily meet a seller.

This is done via liquidity mining, the provision of liquidity.

Currency pairs must always be made available. Below is an example to illustrate the process:

You would like to provide liquidity for $1000.- and therefore buy cryptocurrency A for $500.- and cryptocurrency B for $500.-.

Let's assume you receive 1000 units of currency A and 100 units of currency B.

We therefore know that 10 pieces of currency A cost 1 piece of currency B. The ratio is 10 to 1.

Now someone comes and exchanges currency A for currency B. He pays in 10 units of currency A and receives 1 unit of currency B.

The ratio has therefore changed. The new ratio is 10.01 to 0.99.

There are now, 1010 units of currency A and 99 units of currency B. The total value of $1000 has not changed.

This also means that before the exchange, you could buy 100 units of currency B for the price of 1000 units of currency A.

After the exchange, 99 units of currency B now cost 1010 units of currency A.

The price of currency B has therefore risen in relation to currency A.

Accordingly, it is now advantageous to buy currency A with currency B, as you can now buy 1010 units of currency A for 99 units of currency B.

At this point, another way to make profits comes into play, arbitrage.

As I have already described, you can now buy more currency A with currency B. This restores the original ratio. If you provide liquidity in the form of currency pairs, you earn from the fees charged by the decentralized exchanges for the exchange transactions.

If you engage in arbitrage, you earn from the imbalance of the currency pairs.

Of course, there are also risks here that you need to be aware of. Apart from the risk that the DEX does not work correctly and has errors in the software.

This risk is called impermanent loss. I will not go into the impermanent loss here, as it is a very complex process which, however, evens itself out again after a certain period of time.

It is important to know that you should choose a currency pair that is as correlated as possible. If one currency rises in price, the second currency should also rise. In other words, the relationship between the currency pairs should not fluctuate too much.

The second thing to consider is the period of time in which you carry out liquidity mining. The longer you do it, the lower your risk, as there is enough time for the temporary losses to be recouped with the Fees.

You should also not fixate on a specific date when you want to get out again. There may be an imbalance at precisely this time and you would suffer losses. These could be avoided if you exit a few days later, as the ratios are then balanced again through arbitrage.

As a reminder, if the exchange rate of the two currencies falls, your portfolio will of course also lose value!

If you provide two stablecoins as liquidity, the impermanent loss is negligible, as the two currencies move only minimally apart. For example, USDT (US dollar tether) and USDC (US dollar coin).

In summary, the risks lie in fraudulent exchanges, poor software and imbalances in the currency pairs.

The first two can be avoided through research, the third through time and the right currency pairs.

Now, it would certainly be interesting to find out how high the profits can be with liquidity mining. Depending on the currency pair, between 5% and 110% per year. The less liquidity is made available in a currency pair, the higher your profits and, of course, the higher the risk.

If you are interested in arbitrage, the profits range from 0.5% to 3% per day. However, there are no reputable arbitrage trading providers, so you would have to trade manually, which is very time-consuming.

I hope I have been able to give you a more profound understanding of DeFi and that I have managed to convey the concept to you.

As you have seen, the potential returns are higher than in the traditional financial sector.

In addition, unlike banks, no new currency units are issued when loans are granted.

These are always existing crypto assets that can be invested by saving and forgoing consumption. In addition, the loans granted are always at least 100% collateralized.

However, you must be aware of the risks.

With lending, staking and mining pools, you do not have access to your crypto assets until the term is over.

You therefore have no opportunity to sell your cryptocurrencies if prices plummet.

The time during which your crypto assets are blocked depends on the respective offer. In any case, you must first withdraw your crypto assets from the investment object in order to be able to use them.

You must also be aware that there are no long-established companies involved here. These are all young companies.

As a result, these companies have not yet been able to prove how they will develop over a longer period of time. The risk therefore also lies with the companies themselves.

In June 2022, some of the largest lending platforms collapsed and had to file for bankruptcy. Celsius and Three Arrow Capital were probably the largest. Following the major crash of the crypto markets, these platforms were no longer able to pay out customer funds. Their business model did not work in such extreme markets.

But there is also something good about these bankruptcies. Future lending platforms will pay close attention to what drove these companies into insolvency and avoid these mistakes. This should make lending providers more secure in the future.

Shares and Bonds

You may want to invest in shares or bonds without paying the sometimes high fees charged by conventional stockbrokers or online brokers.

DeFi also offers a solution for this. These are tokenized shares and securities.

These are the aforementioned equity and security tokens. Basically, shares and bonds are digitized. On the one hand, this provides the great advantage that you do not have to buy at least one share. Many shares cost several hundred to over one thousand euros.

For a private investor who can invest three hundred euros a month, it is therefore difficult to buy such shares.

However, this is possible with the Equity and Security Tokens. You pay in around one hundred euros and receive tokens of the desired share or bond in return. As all these tokens have decimal places, you do not have to buy an entire share, but can purchase parts of it. According to your budget and your wishes.

The tokens reflect the exact price performance of the underlying share or bond. However, as you do not own the actual share, you cannot benefit from any dividend payments. You must be aware of this.

However, there are already some changes on the horizon, with companies specifically issuing their own shares in token form. Tokenization results in significantly lower trading fees, and you are not tied to stock exchange opening hours.

In addition, anyone with a smartphone and internet access can participate in the stock markets, ensuring inclusion here too.

Risks

I have already drawn your attention to numerous risks, and would now like to roughly summarize the three most important ones.

The Platform Risk:

This includes all platforms that provide you with a service.

It is not relevant whether this platform offers staking, lending, liquidity mining or digitized shares. All platforms make the complex processes easier for you and ultimately interact with a blockchain.

If this platform does not work properly, your commitment is at stake. You can also run many applications directly on a blockchain yourself. However, this requires in-depth knowledge of exactly how it works and, for example when staking, hardware resources and programming skills.

The Smart Contract Risk:

This risk relates to the quality of the smart contracts used on the blockchain.

If the code is poorly programmed, this can lead to the loss of your investment. It is irrelevant whether you interact directly with the blockchain yourself or use a platform. Please be aware that the platforms also use smart contracts.

The Price Risk:

With most DeFi applications, your crypto assets are locked or blocked.

This can range from a few hours to many months. This is referred to as freezing. During this time, you cannot sell your crypto assets. This means that if, for example, a cryptocurrency loses a significant amount of value, you cannot get out and minimize your losses.

The investment opportunities shown are in no way an investment or purchase recommendation. They are for your information and are only intended to show the possibilities.

Non-Fungible-Token

You may have already heard of NFTs.

In 2020, Christie's auction house auctioned off an NFT for 69 million US dollars. The NFT was produced by Mike Winkelman aka Beeples and bears the name: "Everydays. The first 5000 Days". CryptoPunk # 7523 was auctioned off at Sotheby's in 2021 for 11.8 million US dollars. Both events made it into the mainstream media and news around the globe.

For most people, however, these amounts caused a stunned shake of the head and a complete lack of understanding.

I won't go into these two examples any further, instead you will learn what NFTs are all about and what opportunities they create.

First, let's take a look at what non-fungible actually means:

Non-fungible means that these digital objects are not interchangeable. They are therefore unique.

Currencies are fungible, i.e., interchangeable. If you want to pay for something in the eurozone, it makes no difference whether you use a euro coin from Portugal, Italy, or Germany. This means that the coins are interchangeable or fungible.

Now that we have clarified that, let's move on to the more technical side.

As I wrote at the beginning of the book, values can be transferred on the Web3 and ownership claims can be clearly verified. We have already discussed the transfer of value using a blockchain or DAG.

We also know that these two applications can be used to assign ownership of the respective cryptocurrencies to a wallet. This means that ownership can be clearly verified.

How NFT´s Work

Smart contracts are used here.

These smart contracts are uniquely and unalterably linked to a digital file. This means that you own the file if this smart contract is in your wallet.

Art and Music

Today's distribution channels in the art sector usually run via galleries, auction houses and art dealers.

This means that the majority of the art trade goes through a third party and is restricted in terms of location, for example in the case of galleries.

In addition, it can be difficult to determine the authenticity of a work of art.

In case of doubt, experts must be consulted, who have to check many details to verify authenticity.

Nevertheless, you can never be 100% sure that it is an original. Many counterfeiters have proven that they can fool even proven experts.

The distribution channels in the music industry also run via various third parties. From music labels to retailers and streaming platforms.

With NFTs, artists and musicians have the opportunity to sell their works directly to the end customer.

The only instance in between is the marketplace where the works can be offered. The fees charged by these trading venues are in the lower single-digit percentage range.

The buyer can check the authenticity of the work on the blockchain at any time and has 100% certainty that they have purchased a genuine work.

An additional advantage for the artist are the so-called royalties. When creating the smart contract, the artist can determine what percentage of a future sales price will flow back to them.

In other words, the more often a work is traded and resold, the higher the artist's income via the royalties.

Royalities are used to actively work against royalty infringements and allow artists to participate in resales.

However, the following must be considered with royalties:

At present, the royalties are retained by the exchanges on resale and then transferred to the artist/NFT project. This is still a gentlemen's agreement. It is possible to circumvent the royalties so that the artist does not generate any income from resale. Work is underway to eliminate this shortcoming.

Now let's take a look at how an NFT is created

This process is identical for every NFT. The differences lie in the linked data and the smart contracts that are used.

Let's take a high-resolution photograph with 8000 × 6000 pixels as an example.

As a blockchain cannot store this amount of data, or the storage space would be costly, you upload the image to an external server.

The Inter Planetary File System, IPFS for short, is usually used for this.

IPFS stores the uploaded data on thousands of computers in the network. The data is fragmented, i.e., shredded, and the fragments are divided up and saved on thousands of computers. When the file is accessed, the fragments are reassembled and the entire file is displayed.

As you can see, everything is decentralized here too. The access data for the IPFS file is now added to the smart contract.

Now turn the high-resolution photograph into one with a low resolution. This file serves as a preview and will later be displayed on the desired trading venue.

In a further step, you define the number of NFTs you would like to create. This can be one 1/1 or several 1/50, for example. In the case of art NFTs, it is usually 1/1 or at most low three-digit issues.

For PfP NFTs and collectibles, more on this later, it can be several thousand.

Finally, you need to specify the desired selling price. A smart contract is now programmed from all this data and uploaded to the blockchain.

You can easily do this yourself. All major NFT exchanges offer you this option and guide you through the process step by step.

Each NFT or NFT collection, depending on whether there is only one copy or numerous, has its own smart contract and therefore a unique address. If numerous copies have been created with this smart contract, each copy has a uniquely assigned number or token ID.

You can also link several different files to the same smart contract; these will also have a unique token ID.

Now you only need one buyer.

As you can see, you can use the Smart Contract address to check whether you have an original at any time. It is effortless to determine which Smart Contract was used to create the original, you just have to compare the addresses.

With the music NFTs, the music file is uploaded to IPFS and the record sleeve serves as a preview. Nothing else changes.

NFTs have opened up entirely new distribution channels for artists and musicians.

NFTs also offer the possibility of linking further benefits.

This could be a concert ticket, for example. Anyone who owns an NFT of band X is entitled to a concert ticket. This is integrated into the smart contract to prevent abuse. As soon as the offer has been used, this function is switched off.

This is not a problem and is already used in many other ways.

By purchasing an art or music NFT, you support the artist directly and do not finance intermediaries with your purchase.

Copy/ Paste

One point that skeptics repeatedly raise is the copying of works.

They take the view that if I want the work, I can simply copy it to my computer.

Yes, of course you can do that.

Suppose you buy a Rolex watch for fifty euros on the beach in Ibiza. Can you sell it on to a collector for ten thousand euros?

Probably not, as you only own an almost worthless copy.

You can also copy the Mona Lisa, no problem, but the original will still be hanging in the Louvre and you will have a worthless copy.

The same applies to the picture you have copied onto your computer, it is a worthless copy.

Apart from the legal consequences, you can copy anything, but the copy will never replace the original. The same applies to art and music NFTs, including the legal consequences.

The smart contract and the associated token ID allow you to prove ownership of the original.

P.f.P. and Collectibles

PfP stands for Picture for Profile.

You can use these pictures as profile pictures on Meta, X (Twitter) and all other social media. Collectibles are similar to trading cards or the ever-popular Panini collectible stickers or Baseball Cards.

Before we dive into PfPs and collectibles, I would like to introduce you to a paradigm shift.

CryptoPunks are among the PfPs. As I said at the beginning of the book, a CryptoPunk was auctioned off for over 11 million US dollars. There are some PfP NFTs that went for hundreds of thousands to millions of dollars. There are numerous NFTs that easily reached five-figure sums.

What used to be the sticker of your favorite soccer team is now a PfP. As we move more and more in the virtual space, club badges are becoming less important. In the digital world, group membership is expressed through PfPs.

This puts the 500 or 2000 US dollars that were and are paid for a cheap PfP into perspective. Anyone who supports a sports club or has a favorite car brand knows how much they spend on jerseys, scarves, model cars and other collectibles. The 500-2000 range is quickly reached. But you can't use your collector's items in the virtual world.

Another change is taking place in the area of luxury goods and status symbols.

Be it expensive cars, expensive watches, expensive shoes or handbags. The owners use them to show that they have achieved something and are wealthy.

In the virtual world, CryptoPunks, the Bored Ape Yacht Club, or Pudgy Penguins to name but a few, have replaced these luxury goods and status symbols.

However, some luxury brands have already noticed this trend and are beginning to counteract it.

For example, Alessandro Michele, head designer at Gucci, has launched a PfP collection. He re-dressed well-known PfP NFTs. A Bored Ape Yacht Club NFT with a shirt from Gucci, to name just one example.

I will now introduce you to four PfP projects in more detail. I would like to show you what lies behind these little pictures. You will be amazed at the hidden business models and intentions behind many PfP NFTs.

Encode Graphics

Owner: 0knowlege

Encode Graphics is a project created by Pr1mal Cypher.

Pr1mal Cypher is an NFT artist who has already made a name for himself in the field of NFT art and enjoys a high reputation in the scene.

Encode Graphics works with some of the best-known comic artists, illustrators, and colorists in the industry. Many of the artists work on various DC Comics, Marvel, Star Wars, Doctor Who and many others.

Encode Graphics is associated with a number of comic-related changres. These include the art NFTs, with 1/1 NFTs and other small editions related to the Encode Graphics comics. Then, of course, there are the comics themselves.

Owner: 0knowlege

These are offered as NFTs and physical editions.

In addition, the PfP avatars come from Nexu5 and Leg1on respectively.

Leg1on was created through collaboration with another NFT project, the DystoPunks.

Physical figures from the comics are also planned. As you can see, there is much more to this PfP picture than meets the eye.

Part of the financing came from the Founder Keys. These keys are NFTs that could be minted or bought on the secondary market.

There are bronze, silver and gold keys. Holding one of these keys entitles you to claim Nexu5 PfP NFTs and Leg1on PfPs.

Furthermore, you are entitled to claim every new comic in the form of an NFT.

The cover pages of the comics differ depending on the key. This integrates a rarity; if the comic has been claimed with a Gold Key, it is significantly rarer than one that has been claimed with a Bronze Key.

This can be recognized, as described, on the cover page or the title page.

Gold Key holders will also receive a physical copy of each comic. Silver Key holders will receive a physical yearbook.

Each NFT, whether comic, PfP avatar or 1/1, can be resold on the secondary market. Encode Graphics thus connects the real comic world with the virtual world and expands it with art NFTs, games, and avatars.

Clone X by R.T.F.K.T.

Owner:89DF61

RTFKT, pronounced artifact, is a company that was founded in California in 2020.

The goal was and is to connect the real world with the virtual world. This goal is achieved via NFTs.

Some NFT from RTFKT can be forged. This means that the design of the NFT can be transferred to real sneakers, jackets, or even pieces of jewelry.

Each NFT can only be forged once, so these real products are once again unique. RTFKT has teamed up with manufacturers of these real products and is one of the pioneers when it comes to transferring virtual goods to streetwear and accessories.

RTFKT has also succeeded in inspiring some well-known artists with their ideas. These include Fewocius, Jeff Staple and Takashi Murakami. The game manufacturer ATARI has also launched a sneaker collection with RTFKT.

The original 3D files of all NFTs are made available. This gives NFT owners the opportunity to use their items in augmented reality (AR) and virtual reality (VR).

The images of the NFTs serve as PfP.

With the CloneX collection, RTFKT's largest collection by far with 20,000 NFTs, the boundaries have been pushed a little further.

2972 of these CloneX have a so-called Murakami Drip. These NFTs feature typical attributes of the artist Takashi Murakami.

Another 96 CloneX have the Murakami DNA and were designed almost entirely by Takashi Murakami.

Shortly after the CloneX collection was released, it was announced that RTFKT had been bought by NIKE. The world's largest sports and streetwear manufacturer has thus clearly positioned itself for the extended and virtual world.

Subsequently, every CloneX owner received one SpacePod, per CloneX NFT. A SpacePod is an apartment in the virtual world, developed by oncyber.io. This apartment can be customized by the owner. The simplest way to design it is to hang up your NFTs in the form of pictures. To achieve this, the wallet with the owner's NFTs is connected to the SpacePod and the NFTs in the wallet can be hung up in the SpacePod.

Each SpacePod has its own Internet address so that anyone who has the address can visit the SpacePod. The SpacePods are NFTs in their own right and can be traded on the secondary market.

Some time later, all SpacePod holders received another NFT as a gift, the LootPod. The LootPod is much larger and serves as a kind of gallery. In the LootPod, the owner has more opportunities to present their NFTs. The LootPod is connected to the SpacePod by a door and thus forms a virtual extension of the apartment.

Subsequently, each CloneX holder received an MNLTH, Monolith. The monolith is a cube with the logos of NIKE and RTFKT. To open the monolith, the community had to solve puzzles and tasks for several weeks. When the monolith finally opened in April 2022, it contained another monolith, now the NIKE MNLTH, a pair of white NIKE sneakers and a Skin Vial.

A skin vial is basically the design or surface. This Skin Vial can be inserted into the NIKE sneaker and the standard white sneaker becomes a new shoe with a new design corresponding to the Skin Vial.

These Skin Vials are available in all eight CloneX DNAs. Human, Robot, Angel, Deamon, Reptile Undead, Murakami and Alien. In ascending order of rarity.

The sneakers, the new monolith and the skin vials are also NFTs in their own right and can be traded on the secondary market.

The technology of the skin vials, which is being used here for the first time, opens up entirely new possibilities in augmented and virtual reality.

To put it bluntly, you can imagine it like this:

You only buy one item of clothing at a time. A pair of trousers, a blouse and a pair of shoes. You also have some Skin Vials, which you insert into the desired item of clothing, thus changing the design and appearance of this item of clothing.

Your wardrobe, in terms of the number of items of clothing, will therefore not grow, but can be adapted to fashion trends at any time using the Skin Vials.

No, that's not all. Every CloneX owner whose NFT had a Murakami Drip was given a Murakami Flower designed by Takashi Murakami in the form of an NFT.

In 2023, you could forge the Nike sneaker and thus received the NFT as a real item. By making all 3D models of the CloneX NFTs available, you could modify your own CloneX for all conceivable applications. For example, a CloneX can be used as an avatar in a virtual world or can be modified and customized as desired.

CloneX community members have already developed their own extensions for the Space and LootPods. These range from furniture and decorative items to a complete basketball court for the LootPod.

All these items are NFTs and freely tradable.

Bored Ape Yacht Club

Owner: Choose-me

The Bored Apes were minted in May 2021.

The mint price was 0.08 ETH, which corresponded to around 250 US dollars at the time. The basic idea was to build a media company with NFTs at its core.

Yuga Labs, the publishing company, was founded for this purpose.

The story behind it is about club members who meet in a club and hang around the bar, bored. In the club's restroom, there is a pin board on which messages could be pinned. The club became a yacht club and the members are the bored apes. The Bored Ape Yacht Club was born.

Initially, sales were very slow. The Bored Apes had already been minted for a few days, but were still a long way from selling all 10,000 Apes.

Pranksy, a well-known NFT collector and trader, minted some of these new apes and spread the word via X (formerly known as Twitter), and 12 hours later the apes were sold out. All it took was one influencer to give the project a boost.

Whether Pranksy was contacted by Yuga Labs or not has been the subject of much debate. Both Pranksy and Yuga Labs. deny any communication before purchase.

It was helpful for the spread of the monkeys that many well-known personalities bought a monkey.

These include Jimmy Fallon, Paris Hilton, Eminem and many other stars.

Yuga Labs published a roadmap right from the start. A roadmap is nothing more than a kind of business plan that shows what is to be introduced and implemented along the timeline.

Yuga Labs stuck to this roadmap and worked through and implemented the points step by step. As a result, Yuga Labs gained the trust of NFT holders and rewarded this trust with additional benefits.

One of the most important benefits for holders of BAYC NFTs are the rights that come with them. Each holder has full commercial rights to their NFTs. This means that a holder can use his NFT as a company logo, he can make and sell clothing with the image of his NFTs, he can rent out his NFT and so on.

Other advantages were so-called airdrops. With an airdrop, new NFTs or coins are transferred to the respective wallet for all eligible holders.

For the BAYC holders, these were dog NFTs, the Bored Ape Kennel Club. Then there was the serum, the Bored Ape Chemistry Club, so to speak. Finally, the APE Coins were added.

A new technology was introduced with the Chemistry Club serums, M1 and M2, where M stands for mutate. Figuratively speaking, you administer a serum to your monkey that causes it to mutate. The result is a new NFT that can still recognize the original NFT, but is completely disfigured. These new NFTs belong to the Mutant Ape Yacht Club, or MAYC for short.

Owner: C549F6

Around the twentieth of March 2022, all holders of BAYC and MAYC received an airdrop of the APE Coin.

The APE Coin was distributed to the owners of Bored Apes and Mutant Apes. If the respective owner still held a Kennel Club NFT, he received correspondingly more APE Coins.

The APE Coin is the internal currency in the Ape universe. Promotional items such as shirts, hoodies etc. can be purchased with APE. They also have the right to vote.

The virtual properties of the Apes could also be minted with APE.

The Otherside with the Otherdeeds refers to the virtual world of the Apes and their properties. The Otherdeeds were not given to the owners by airdrop. The holders were given a right of first refusal on high-value properties.

But the story doesn't end with the additional NFTs and coins.

A record label of the Universal Music Group founded the band KINGSHIP, consisting of a Mutant Ape and three Bored Apes. The virtual band is based on the GORILLAS, the world's first commercially successful virtual band.

With Bored and Hungry, Andy Nguyen opened a fast-food restaurant in Long Beach, California. A Bored Ape and three Mutant Apes are used as company logos. These can be found on the drink's cups, napkins, hamburger boxes and, of course, on the roof of the restaurant. In addition to US dollars, you can pay with Ethereum/ ETH or APE Coin. Originally, the restaurant was only planned as a pop-up for three months. Due to its great success, it will now remain open permanently.

Coinbase, the world's largest crypto exchange, is in the process of filming a three-part series with the Bored Apes. This involves three short films with the Bored Apes as actors. Degen Trilogy is the name of the project. Degen or Degenerate is the name given in the NFT scene to someone who simply invests in NFTs without any research or information. A so-called degen play is therefore a high-risk investment that is really just based on hype and word of mouth.

Owners of BAYC NFTs can submit their monkeys for casting or auditions. If a monkey gets a role in the trilogy, the owner will be remunerated.

As you can see, there is much more to the Bored Apes than just pictures of bored monkeys. It will be very exciting to see what will emerge from the Yacht Club.

Pudgy Penguins

Owner: Betthoever

The Pudgy Penguins were created during the hype phase of NFTs in 2021.

The NFT project was very successful at the time and was able to become an established, profitable and stable project relatively quickly.

It is now May 2023 and the Pudgy Penguins have landed another coup. No less a company than Walmart is working with the NFT project.

The Pudgy Penguins are being brought onto the market by Walmart as real stuffed animals. Each stuffed animal has a digital twin in the form of an NFT. Owners of the Pudgy Penguins NFTs receive a share of the revenue from the stuffed animals.

The NFT in turn allows access to Pudgy World. There is a lot to discover in this virtual world, be it small games, new information or simply a chat with like-minded people.

According to the Pudgy Penguins team, Pudgy World is still in its infancy and will gradually offer more applications.

In addition to the options and applications mentioned above, the Pudgy Penguins rely on a strong and committed community. Following the announcement of the Walmart deal, NFT prices have risen again significantly.

Scam and Fraud

But there are also downsides to the PfP and collectible sector.

Due to the exceptionally high profits that can be made, more and more fraudsters are getting a taste for it.

You must be aware that the PfP and collectibles market is unfortunately still like the Wild West. Recently, more and more fraudsters have been prosecuted and brought to justice.

This has mainly happened in the United States of America. From fraud to insider trading, numerous offenses were prosecuted and punished.

However, when it comes to PfP NFTs and collectibles, we are operating in a global market and therefore in a wide variety of jurisdictions with more or less strict rules. This means that there are still plenty of loopholes for fraudsters.

In such a market, you have to take care of your security.

This starts with the use of VPNs, virtual private networks. A VPN masks your IP address and therefore your location. It also makes it more difficult for hackers to access your computer, as these accesses often run via your IP address. If the IP address changes at relatively short intervals, it becomes more difficult for hackers to maintain access.

Another important step is direct messaging on X (formerly known as Twitter), Telegram, and Discord. All of these platforms are used to talk about PfP NFTs and collectibles. If you follow a Twitter channel or are registered on a server on Discord that deals with NFTs, there is a high risk that scammers will send you fraudulent website links via direct messages. You should therefore block all direct messages from people you do not know. This significantly reduces the risk of you clicking on a fraudulent link.

You must always be aware that with a blockchain, there is no support or helpdesk that you can call if you have made a mistake. Once you confirm a transaction, your funds are gone. If you grant a smart contract access to your wallet, your balance and all the NFTs it contains are gone.

Now that you've read about the dangers, let's move on to other uses for non-fungible tokens. I'm pretty sure you'll discover some applications you hadn't thought of.

Gaming NFTs

The games NFTs are, as the name suggests, used in online games.

These can be avatars, items or plots of land.

To understand the purpose of these NFTs, let me take a step back and show you how conventional online games like World of Warcraft work.

In WoW, you log in and choose a character. This can be a wizard or a warrior, for example. Now, you explore the world of WoW with your character or avatar. During your explorations, you may find items that you can collect or fight against various opponents and receive useful items or weapons if you win.

You also have the option of buying items from a merchant, which you pay for with gold. WoW gold serves as a means of payment.

There are many players who earn euros and dollars playing WoW by selling characters/avatars. These players started with a new avatar and played until this avatar became stronger and better.

The improved avatar can now be sold on eBay. Once this is done, the player starts again with a new avatar and improves it by playing WoW and also sells this improved avatar once more.

However, there are two problems with this: All items and avatars do not belong to the respective player. If the game developer discontinues the game or changes the rules, the players automatically lose everything.

Selling on eBay leaves too many opportunities for fraudsters. This could mean that the seller does not deliver the avatar or that the buyer, once he has the avatar, demands his money back via PayPal.

This is where NFTs come into play. If the issuer removes the game from the internet, the players still have their NFTs in their wallets. Smart contracts make reselling much more secure for everyone involved.

You may now be wondering what the advantage is if a game is discontinued, and you only have the NFTs left?

These would then be worthless. Apart from the fact that they can still be collector's items, you are of course right, but. ENJIN is a platform that allows game developers to publish games.

The great thing about it is that NFTs can be used in different games.

For example, you received a golden sword in game A. This golden sword is now in your wallet as an NFT. Let's say in game A the golden sword has more destructive power and deals more damage to the opponent per blow.

On ENJIN you can also use this sword in game B, possibly increasing your spell power in game B.

So, you can see that your NFTs can be used across games. As you log in to the respective games with your wallet, you can also use the NFTs contained in the wallet across games.

So, it is no tragedy if a game no longer exists.

TREASURE DAO works similarly on the Arbitrum blockchain. All Treasure DAO online games use the MAGIC coin as currency. In Treasure DAO games, it is often possible to switch games with an avatar. Various items can also be used across games. These types of use were first made possible by blockchain technology and wallets, which significantly expanded the application possibilities for online games.

Which brings us to P2E, play to earn or play to earn.

There are already quite a few P2E games. The aim can be, similar to World of Warcraft, that you improve an avatar and sell it or sell items that you have found or won. These can also be strategy games, similar to SimCity, in which you build and operate houses, factories, power stations or waterworks. The land on which you build is an NFT and is yours. The products you manufacture are NFTs and belong to you. The buildings are also NFTs and naturally also are yours. Everything can be traded via marketplaces.

The smarter you use your buildings and land, the higher your yield and your real income. MEGA CRYPTO POLIS is such a strategy game and runs on the Ethereum, TRON and Binance blockchain. Your winnings are paid out in Ethereum, Tron or BNB, which you can easily exchange for euros, US dollars or Swiss francs via an exchange.

This has created entirely new sources of income, and many Web3 enthusiasts are now making a relatively good living from gaming.

There are also constant updates on the technical side. For example, a new type of smart contract has been introduced on the Ethereum blockchain.

With the ERC 6551 smart contract, a wallet can be inextricably linked to each NFT. This means that your avatar's NFT has its own wallet in which all items or coins that have been earned are stored. This offers great advantages when transferring or selling the avatar. You send the avatar and the recipient gains access to all items in the linked wallet.

This new standard, which was introduced in 2022, also opens up new application possibilities beyond gaming NFTs.

In the area of digital identities, your entire professional career can now be linked to your identity.

Tickets

Tickets are another use case for NFTs.

At the final match of the Champions League in Paris 2022, there was a medium-sized scandal as many fans of the Reds (Liverpool FC) were not allowed into the stadium even though they had valid tickets.

Frustrated and angry, the fans stood outside the stadium throughout the final match. Apart from the financial damage caused to these fans by the ticket price and travel, the reputation of the stadium operators and UEFA took a significant blow.

One of the main problems was counterfeit tickets that did not work at the turnstiles, causing significant congestion and resentment among those in line. This issue can be solved with NFTs.

Another advantage of NFTs as tickets is that they can be resold securely, as their authenticity can be verified at any time. In addition, the issuer could earn money from the resale through royalties. The resale prices can also be actively influenced by setting the maximum resale price. This makes it unattractive for professional gangs to sell tickets on the black market, and hoarding can be controlled.

As a result, more tickets would be available to fans at the regular price.

Other possibilities linked to the NFTs could be a discount on the purchase of fan merchandise or the raffle of pre-match stadium tours among NFT holders. It would also be possible to give all NFT holders an NFT as a thank you after the game. For example, a jersey of the winning team to wear in a virtual world.

As you can see, the possibilities are almost unlimited, but always require a real NFT and therefore a valid ticket.

Another option is the so-called POAPs, Proof of Attendance Protocol. I will also discuss POAPs in more detail later in the book.

Access to Content and Applications

Similar to tickets, content, applications, and services on the internet can also be controlled using NFTs.

The possibilities range from news sites in a wide variety of media to applications and tools, including analytics applications, to content for professionals and experts.

In Web2, you had to create an account for each website, service, and application. A separate password for each account and possibly a fee to use the service. If you have paid a subscription fee and only want to use the service for a short time, the fee is no longer applicable.

Web3 makes this much easier and cheaper. For accounts that do not require a subscription payment, you log in with your digital wallet. The application will only remember the public key, and you can log in again at any time with the corresponding wallet.

If you want to use a fee-based offer, buy the respective NFT.

The NFT can grant you lifelong or time-limited access.

You now reconnect your wallet to the desired website. The website will check whether you are in possession of the relevant NFT and activate the offers for you.

Firstly, this is completely anonymous and secondly, you don't have to create a new account every time. This means you don't have to write down hundreds of different passwords.

A decisive advantage lies in the resale of the NFT. You do not have to cancel your subscription; you simply sell your NFT. This means you don't pay regular subscription fees that are gone for good, but you pay once for an NFT that gives you lifelong access. If you no longer use the offer, you will get at least part of your expenses back by selling it.

If demand for the offer increases, NFT prices may even rise if the NFTs are limited. Ideally, you could use the offer for a longer period of time and then resell the NFT at a profit.

Incidentally, this is not utopian, but happens regularly in the NFT scene. These are often so-called alpha groups. These groups analyze NFT projects. They take a close look at the team and what the team members have already successfully implemented. The business model is analyzed, and it is determined whether there is a market for it.

In short, the Alpha Groups determine the fundamentals of the project and summarize them. These summaries in turn serve as the basis for investment decisions. As this work is extremely time-consuming and requires an excellent network, this data is only passed on to NFT owners.

The better the analyses in these Alpha Groups are and the more profit opportunities arise from these analyses, the higher the price on the secondary market for the Alpha Group's NFTs.

There are also various analysis applications that are activated using NFTs. In these applications, for example, all sales are displayed on a timeline. This allows trends to be identified and possible purchase options to be tracked down. Digital wallets of well-known collectors are tracked. For example, if Pranksy buys NFTs from a collection, this could be a sign that the price of these NFTs will rise.

In these applications, different data is processed and displayed in graphical representations. They therefore serve as an aid in the search for interesting NFT projects and investment opportunities.

As I mentioned at the beginning, this approach can be applied to a wide variety of applications. Access to the latest medical studies for doctors. Current building regulations for craftsmen or up-to-date manuals for mechatronics engineers.

All this and much more can be managed with NFTs.

Decentralized Digital Identities

DIDs are similar to the above-mentioned access options to services and Internet platforms.

DID stand for Decentralized Identifier Document. Here, your data is checked for authenticity by a central company or authority and then stored in your wallet. This verified data can also be used for applications that require a Know Your Customer (KYC) procedure.

The KYC procedure is required, for example, when registering with a regulated crypto exchange. This is a verification of the customer, similar to the data you have to provide when you open a bank account.

It's basically about the regulatory requirements of the relevant authorities.

Now, let's assume you want to enter a trendy club in the city center. The club is open to people aged 18 and over, and the doorman would like to know if you are of the appropriate age.

You will show the doorman your passport or driving license to prove your age. The problem with this is that your name, date of birth and possibly, your address are written on this ID document, i.e., all details that are not actually relevant for the bouncer.

With a DID, the bouncer would ask whether you are 18 years old and the DID would answer yes or no.

The bouncer would therefore have requested and checked the desired information without seeing any other data.

With this small example, I wanted to make it clear to you that you often disclose too much data, although this is not absolutely necessary.

Depending on the KYC requirement for a service, the provider may not need to collect and manage data records. They only need to be able to prove that the customer meets all the requirements. This is done via requests similar to the bouncer.

It is not necessary for the provider to check the data itself again, as it has already received a yes or no from the wallet in response to the corresponding requests.

This means that the provider only has to store the wallet addresses of its customers, in which the required data is stored in encrypted form. This helps with compliance with the GDPR, the General Data Protection Regulation, as the merchant no longer has to store this data.

Another advantage is that you can be paid for your data.

You all know the problems with today's data black holes like Google and Facebook. Your data is sold or used to optimize the advertising messages sent to you.

In short, someone is making money from your data.

With a DID it is possible to earn money yourself if you disclose your data or parts of it.

The following example illustrates this:

You would like to buy a new car. You have configured your desired vehicle on the manufacturer's website and would like to receive an offer for the vehicle from various dealers. Furthermore, you place your vehicle request and your wallet address on an internet platform. Every dealer who wants to make you an offer pays an amount to your wallet using a smart contract and receives your name, address, and email address from your wallet in return.

By disclosing your data, you have generated an income and the dealers can make you a precise offer for your desired vehicle.

The result is a win-win situation. The dealer does not have to spend a lot of time asking how the vehicle should be configured and receives a potential new customer via the platform.

As a customer, your data is paid for, and you receive offers for your desired vehicle. The whole process has become more effective and time-saving for both sides.

One objection could be that anyone can then configure countless vehicles and request offers each time to earn money from their data.

This may work for a short period of time. As the data is read from the respective wallet and the wallet address is therefore known, blacklists will quickly be established among car dealers and requests from these wallets will be ignored or even reported.

Contracts and Agreements

Thanks to blockchain technology and smart contracts, all contracts, agreements, and arrangements can also be stored transparently.

Transparent and tamper-proof storage is particularly important for government agreements. This can promote the population's trust in the government, as all contracts and agreements can be viewed by any citizen at any time.

In this case, it is also an NFT in the broadest sense, as each smart contract has its address and the contract pages are provided with a unique identification number within the smart contract. This makes it clear how many pages the document has.

P.O.A.P.

POAPs are another area of NFTs.

POAP stands for Proof of Attendance Protocol.

POAPs could be used to verify attendance at a training course, for example. The entire professional career can therefore be mapped using POAPs. When applying for a job, only the wallet address with the saved POAPs needs to be entered, so the recruiter has a complete overview of the candidate's education and training.

POAPs can also be used in conjunction with admission tickets. As soon as the digital ticket has been validated, a POAP is sent to the address on the ticket. This allows the holder to prove that they were present at the World Cup final, for example.

It is also possible to link additional offers and benefits to the POAPs. To stay tuned for the World Cup final, the holder can purchase a final jersey for their team upon presentation of the POAP or receive a right of first refusal on tickets for the next World Cup.

As you can see, POAPs can also be used to generate countless opportunities.

This ranges from customer loyalty to a "thank you" to a complete career in your professional environment.

As POAPs are also stored on a blockchain using a smart contract, they are protected against manipulation and their authenticity can be verified at any time.

POAPs are basically NFTs and based on a smart contract. This could enable resale. The offers and benefits associated with a POAP would therefore be freely tradable.

The issuer of the POAPs can participate in the resale via the royalties.

Collateral

An acquaintance of mine works at the OeNB, the Austrian National Bank.

One of his tasks is to develop blockchain applications for the banking and central bank sector. I was amazed that a conservative and rather crypto-skeptical organization like the Austrian central bank is working on developing blockchain-based applications.

One of the potential use cases that the OeNB is testing is NFTs that serve as collateral for loans.

Many banks, especially those in the South, hold works of art as collateral for loans and credits. Handling such collateral is time-consuming and cost-intensive. Storage, transportation, and verification of authenticity by external experts, to name but a few.

In addition, the credit or loan can only be paid out once the authenticity of the artwork has been confirmed.

Now, let's assume that you own a valuable painting that is on display in a museum. The museum has already verified its authenticity for insurance purposes. Now you need short-term liquidity and would like to lend your work of art and deposit it as collateral for a loan.

As mentioned above, this is expensive.

Now let's assume that there is a unique digital image of your painting in the form of an NFT. This NFT thus verifies ownership of the real work of art. Now you send your NFT to the bank and thus transfer ownership to the bank. The bank can transfer your loan amount to you immediately upon receipt of the NFT.

The artwork does not have to be transported from the museum, nor does its authenticity have to be verified again. All time, transportation, and storage costs are eliminated, and the transaction can be completed in just a few minutes.

Dynamic NFTs

You may have noticed something in the examples shown above.

The underlying smart contracts cannot be changed. If you wanted to change something, the entire smart contract would have to be reprogrammed. This would be impractical with the decentralized digital identity, for example. A new smart contract would always have to be written if there was a change of residence or additional training. This is where dynamic NFTs come into play.

The underlying smart contracts can be adjusted. The degree and type of customization are firmly anchored in the smart contract.

As an example, let's take an NFT that shows a landscape image.

If it is raining in your region on this day, the NFT image will also show a rainy landscape. If the sun is shining in your region, the sun will also shine on your NFT landscape image.

In this example, the smart contract would receive the weather information via a so-called oracle. You will learn more about oracles later. The NFT adapts to changing conditions via the dynamic smart contract.

A change of residence or new additional training in your decentralized digital identity is no longer a problem and is simply updated in the existing smart contract.

This technology enables other very exciting use cases.

Non Transferable Token

Another difficulty that you may have discovered is the transfer option, as long as you hold the private keys to your wallet.

This option is not desirable for your digital, decentralized identity. It is not relevant whether you want to transfer your identity intentionally or accidentally.

Non-transferable NFTs are therefore another important component of NFTs.

Dangers

I have already pointed out the dangers posed by fraudsters.

Further dangers lurk in the hacking of entire NFT ecosystems.

In such a case, you as the owner of an NFT are almost powerless, as it is not your wallet that is attacked, but the application itself.

Unfortunately, this happens again and again and users are not always compensated.

One of the most active hacker groups is Lazarus, which works for North Korea. This group has also been increasingly attacking Web3 applications since 2018.

Another type of danger comes from the hype surrounding individual projects. These projects are promoted by influencers and well-known personalities. This creates the illusion that the project in question is particularly innovative, valuable, or popular.

As a result, projects can experience enormous short-term increases in value, only to disappear into oblivion after a hype phase.

Parallels to stock markets can be observed here.

In the technology bubble at the end of the 1990s, a new company only had to have dot com in its name and thus had a real chance of making a lot of money.

Whether the advertised application behind it was useful or not was often of secondary importance. Something similar happened in the crypto scene in 2017: the ICO hype.

ICO stands for Initial Coin Offering, which is basically nothing more than project financing.

At that time, mainly Ethereum was transferred to the project and in return, you received the respective project token. It was actually a virtual IPO. Projects and applications such as Filecoin, Tezos and EOS still exist today. These projects have developed into companies that generate added value and launched products that are used.

Without having exacted figures, I estimate that around 99 percent of the ICOs at the time have disappeared, and the respective tokens are worthless.

I would rather not demonize the dot com bubble and the ICO hype and portray it as unnecessary or even criminal.

Quite the opposite.

These phases separated the wheat from the chaff and helped a new technology achieve a breakthrough. In the end, companies and applications developed from this that are still very successful today. Amazon, Google, PayPal and eBay, to name just a few.

It is only necessary to understand that Web3 is still in the discovery phase and that there is a lot of experimentation going on. Much will disappear again and some will remain. What remains will once again cause major upheavals.

I hope I have been able to make you understand the concept and possible dangers of the various NFT applications.

I am fully aware that there will be further possible applications in the future and that more applications will be found, but the examples shown should suffice as an overview.

In the next chapter, I will introduce you to social coins and some application examples.

Social-Coins and D.A.O.

The first question we need to answer is: "What are social coins?"

A social coin, originally derived from social media, is a way for influencers to strengthen their brand and bind subscribers more closely to the brand.

Basically, a social coin is the currency that an influencer issues. The subscribers and holders of these social coins can use the social coins to pay for the influencer's goods or services.

There are several platforms that make such social coins possible. MintMe uses the Bitcoin blockchain, while Roll and Rally run on the Ethereum blockchain. Anyone can generate their own cryptocurrency on these platforms.

Usually, 10 million coins are created, which are issued over a defined period of time. Everyone can choose whether all 10 million coins are available from the outset, or whether the issue should be spread over 10 years.

The social coins are freely tradable on the respective platforms and can be exchanged for Ethereum or Bitcoin at any time.

One popular application of these social coins is SOCIOS with the Chilli token. SOCIOS has set itself the goal of bringing supporters of sports clubs or motorsport teams closer to their favorite club or team.

Clubs and teams such as FC Barcelona, Chicago Bulls, San Francisco 49ers, Anaheim Ducks and Aston Martin Cognizant F1, to name but a few, are represented on SOCIOS and allow their fans to influence the teams. This can be the choice of the new jerseys, the inscription on the captain's armband, the design of the dressing rooms and much more.

Which brings us to an exciting application, the DAOs.

D.A.O.

Decentral Autonomus Organization.

To give you an understanding of the concept of a DAO, here is an example:

A company that produces smartphone apps creates its own social coin, let's call it AppCoin. Anyone who purchases an app from this company receives ten percent of the purchase price in the form of AppCoins transferred to their wallet.

The customer can use these AppCoins to purchase future apps or updates from this company. So far, the AppCoin is similar to a voucher or a discount stamp.

But the AppCoin can do even more.

AppCoin holders can vote on changes or suggest changes. For example, an AppCoin holder would like to be able to switch the background of the app to black. They enter this suggested change and the other AppCoin holders can vote on it. If the proposal is accepted, the issuing company knows what the customers want and can integrate the update in the next app version.

This is where we see the first advantage for the issuing company. The company knows exactly what the customers want, which reduces the risk of misguided developments and the associated costs.

But that is by no means all.

The issuing company pays a small part of the employees' salaries in AppCoins. The AppCoin can be used by employees as a means of payment in the canteen or at the coffee machine. An upgrade for the next company car for employees could also be paid for with the AppCoin.

The important thing is that employees have the opportunity to use their AppCoins.

You may be wondering what this is all about.

Let's take a closer look at the tensions within a company today.

The management wants to generate as much profit as possible. Accordingly, it intends to sell its products as expensively as possible and at the same time pay its employees as little as possible in the form of salaries.

The employees would like to work as little as possible and earn as much as possible at the same time.

The customer, on the other hand, wants to pay as little as possible and receive as much as possible for what they pay for.

As you can see, the needs and wishes of all parties involved go in entirely different directions. This creates friction and conflicts.

Now let's take a closer look at the example of the AppCoin.

The customer wants the AppCoin to be as valuable as possible in terms of the local currency. This means they have to pay less AppCoin for future updates or new apps.

Employees also want the AppCoin to be as valuable as possible, as this allows them to consume more in the canteen. An increase in the value of the AppCoin is equivalent to a salary increase.

The management also wants the AppCoin to increase in value. Firstly, they can also use it in the canteen and secondly, a rising AppCoin price attracts new customers. It also reduces the risk of unnecessary expenditure on undesirable developments. The more customers use the AppCoin, the more targeted the updates or new apps can be developed.

With the introduction of the AppCoin, the following has now happened. Everyone involved is working in the same direction. Everyone wants AppCoin to increase in value.

You can introduce a DAO just for individual products, like our app, or build an entire company on it.

Decentraland, one of the largest virtual worlds, more on this later, is designed as a DAO. In Decentraland, the community determines the majority of the smart contracts used and influences a wide variety of attributes and practices in Decentraland. These include, to name just a few, the options for landowners, the amount of marketplace fees, which new items of clothing can be implemented and the election or deselection of members of the Security Board.

After the development of Decentraland, these rights and options were gradually handed over to the community.

If you take this idea further, you come to the conclusion that an entire country can theoretically be governed with a DAO.

In this chapter, I have tried to give you an understanding of social coins and the concept of DAOs. I hope I have been able to give you an idea of what is possible with them.

Metaverse

We all remember the lockdowns during the coronavirus pandemic well.

Due to curfews and access restrictions, a considerable part of the economy shifted online. People worked from home and meetings were held via Zoom conferencing. Entire trade fairs and congresses were held virtually on people's own computer screens. Pupils' and students' lessons also moved online. Depending on the degree of digitalization, this worked better in some countries and worse in others.

In addition, concerts, vernissages and many other events did not take place or had to be canceled. As a result, not only was professional life severely affected, but private life was also severely impacted by curfews.

This had serious economic consequences on the one hand and social and personal consequences on the other.

This is where the various online offerings came into play. The Zoom conference on the more professional and educational side, and the virtual worlds on the more private side.

What?

Some of you will remember Second Life.

Second Life allowed users to engage in virtual commerce using the Linden Dollar as a means of payment. Others met in Second Life to spend time together, and companies used Second Life for meetings. For international companies in particular, it was much easier and cheaper to bring employees together in Second Life than to fly them to the headquarters.

Another widespread application is gaming. Regardless of whether these are consoles or online games. There, too, you enter a virtual world and interact with your fellow players or opponents. Information, strategies or simply small talk are exchanged there using a chat function (written) or with a headset (acoustic).

The problem with all of these applications, as I already mentioned in the Game's NFTs section, is that you are not the owner of the avatars and items. You are therefore dependent on the game operator.

Of course, you could argue that if a decentralized game or virtual world goes offline, everything becomes worthless because it can no longer be used. It doesn't matter whether I own the item or have just borrowed it.

That is perfectly correct for now. However, a closer look reveals some crucial differences:

- The balance earned is a cryptocurrency that can be exchanged for another cryptocurrency or fiat currency at any time.

- All assets are NFTs and can therefore be freely traded at any time.

- In Decentraland and The Sandbox, to name just two of the best-known virtual worlds, property, and currency owners have a say. For many planned changes, the community decides whether they are introduced or not.

As you can see, there are some crucial differences between whether a virtual world is centralized or decentralized via a blockchain.

Of course, it is the same with decentralized virtual worlds: if nobody uses them, they will disappear. The important thing, however, is that supply and demand are at work here.

Now let's take a look at the possibilities of virtual worlds. Broadly speaking, we can categorize the applications as follows, whereby any kind of hybrid form is possible.

- Replacement or extension of social media.

- Presentation of companies-in the broadest sense, a walk-in website.

- Game-oriented virtual worlds.

- Business-oriented applications for meetings and conferences.

- Exhibitions and galleries.

- Sale of virtual/digital and real goods.

- Concerts and cultural events.

Replacement or Extension of Social-Media

Social media is an example of an application for virtual worlds.

In Web2, participants communicate on Facebook/ Meta, LinkedIn and other platforms. The exchange takes place in writing via posts and comments.

In a virtual world, the participants meet with their avatars and can communicate with each other in writing or acoustically via microphone and loudspeaker.

Contributions with photos or videos are shown on surfaces, similar to posters or video walls, in the respective groups. The participants can now discuss and talk about what they have seen on the spot, so to speak. The idea of social media has not changed, but additional options have been added.

Presentation of Companies

Companies have the opportunity to set up a branch in the virtual worlds, in effect a walk-in website.

The company can offer a wide variety of services and information in this branch. For example, it is possible to sell subscriptions to online services via NFTs or to present the company's own product range.

A help or service function for customers is also easy to implement.

Depending on where this store is located, it can also lead to walk-in customers in the virtual world.

Assuming your retail store is located in a city in Austria, you are limited to customers in your region. You can expand your customer base through online trading, provided the customers know your company.

However, you will only get regular customers and therefore new customers from the vicinity of your location.

With a branch in the virtual world, you can present your company worldwide. With walk-in customers in the virtual world, you are no longer limited to your region.

Game-Oriented Worlds

Imagine a games room in the 80s and 90s.

There were rows and rows of pinball machines and arcade games. There were racing games such as OutRun or games of skill like Pac-Man or Donkey Kong.

At the same time, these gaming salons were also a meeting place. People talked about new games, high scores, the new bike, in short, about God and the world.

Virtual worlds offer this opportunity in the digital age. As a property owner, you can program (or have programmed) a game on your property and monetize it. As a player, you move around in this world and play whatever you feel like. You can exchange ideas with other players and find out where a new game is currently on offer.

You can also meet with friends and discover new games together and chat about the world.

Business-Oriented Worlds

Employees from international companies, for example, meet in these virtual worlds.

These virtual worlds offer many opportunities for presentations, lectures, exchanging ideas or internal company communication. Employees are present via microphone, loudspeaker, and screen. Films, live videos or presentations are transmitted directly into the virtual meeting room.

By connecting a microphone and loudspeaker, it is possible to hold an acoustic exchange of ideas or a discussion, similar to a Zoom meeting.

Exhibitions and Galleries

Exhibitions, trade fairs and galleries are another possible application.

Objects can be displayed there in the form of NFTs or three-dimensional models. Companies can thus present a wide range of prototypes or objects that have already been developed. This gives interested parties the opportunity to obtain information in advance and view the objects in three-dimensional space.

In the art sector, works of art are shown in the form of NFTs. These can be museums or galleries that specialize in a wide variety of styles.

Sale of Virtual, Digital and Real Goods

To stay on the subject of art.

Sotheby's, one of the best-known auction houses, has a branch in Decentraland. The front façade of the London headquarters has been recreated. Sotheby's organizes auctions in the branch and auctions NFT works of art in Decentraland.

Of course, galleries can also offer the NFTs on display for sale directly from the virtual world. This is also already widespread. Some galleries deliver the real artwork to the buyer after the purchase of an NFT.

Another possible application is wearables for avatars. These are items of clothing or accessories for the avatars in this virtual world. Nike, Gucci and several other brands are already experimenting with such clothing and accessories.

T-shirt for Decentraland avatar

Concerts and Cultural Events

During the 2020 and 2021 lockdowns, entire music festivals took place in Decentraland.

DJs and bands were projected in sound and vision onto a stage in Decentraland. Viewers were able to watch a music festival from their screens. Using a microphone and loudspeaker, it was also possible to chat with your neighbor.

The same is easily possible with plays, operas, operettas, and all other stage productions. The performance is captured on the real stage using image and sound technology and projected directly into the virtual world.

This allows visitors from all over the world to watch the play. As cameras are already used to display the video walls, primarily at large open-air events, the technical effort involved in projecting these images into a virtual world is relatively straightforward. The technical equipment such as microphones, cameras, and control rooms are already on site anyway.

All you need is internet access and the streaming hardware to play the virtual worlds.

The examples above have given you a small selection of the possibilities. I am absolutely certain that you, dear reader, will spontaneously think of many other possibilities.

Of course, a virtual world in no way replaces a meeting or event in real life, nor is that the aim.

However, they do provide access to events for people who cannot attend real-life meetings and events because they live on the other side of the world, for example.

From a business perspective, branches in the virtual world are an evolution of company websites.

It remains to be seen how the virtual worlds will develop and whether they will be accepted by the public.

The foundation stone has been laid.

On the Bitcoin Blockchain?

All the applications shown work and are operated on smart contract-capable networks. The question that arises is, does this also work on the Bitcoin network?

Yes, at least partially.

Inscription and Ordinals

This is where the so-called inscriptions come into play.

A network update at the end of 2022 made it possible to attach information to the Satoshi´s.

Satoshi´s are the smallest unit of Bitcoin, the Bitcoin cents, so to speak. As Bitcoin has eight decimal places, 100 million satoshis equal one Bitcoin. The update became known as Taproot.

As the storage space on the Bitcoin blockchain is limited to a maximum of 4 MB per block, the files attached to the Satoshis are also limited.

Function:

As already mentioned, files are attached to a Satoshi.

This is done via Taproot-enabled wallets and applications. In addition, each of these inscriptions is numbered consecutively. This makes it possible to create and trade NFTs on the Bitcoin blockchain.

On the other hand, new crypto coins can also be implemented. These are described as BRC 20. The NFTs are ordinals. The name is based on the Ethereum smart contract standards. ERC 20 are fungible assets on the Ethereum blockchain. In other words, crypto coins, like the USDC.

The BRC 20 coins are each attached to a Satoshi. The Satoshi´s are also numbered consecutively. When the ordinals or BRC 20 coins are transferred, the Satoshi`s to which the inscription is attached are basically moved.

However, this requires wallets in which you can select and send the desired Satoshi´s. These special wallets must be Taproot-capable.

Difference to NFTs

As I described above, NFTs are external files that are linked to a smart contract. This means that the files are not stored on the blockchain. (With a few exceptions) In the case of ordinals, all files are stored on the Bitcoin blockchain as they are directly attached to a Satoshi.

Smart-Contracts on Bitcoin

Smart contracts are possible directly on the Bitcoin blockchain. However, as the storage capacities are so small, this makes little sense.

This is where the second layer, layer 2, comes into play. There are two different approaches. A new programming language and existing programming language.

STACKS

STACKS uses its own programming language and processes the smart contracts on its own blockchain and stores the result on the Bitcoin blockchain. This means that STACKS, like all other Layer 2s, uses the main network to secure the results.

ROOTSTOCK

ROOTSTOCK uses the Ethereum smart contracts. Like many other blockchains, ROOTSTOK is EVM (Ethereum virtual machine) capable. This comes with the advantage that an existing smart contract standard can be used.

In addition, existing applications can be accessed. ROOTSTOCK also stores the transaction results on the Bitcoin blockchain.

The Outcry in the Bitcoin Community

The Bitcoin maximalists, recognizable by the laser eyes on their profile pictures, are and were anything but pleased about the new possibilities.

They see the Bitcoin network as an exclusive payment network and Bitcoin as the only legitimate cryptocurrency.

They see everything else as shit coins.

They fear that the new possibilities will overload the network and result in a massive increase in transaction fees. This is precisely what happened at the beginning of 2023, when more and more ordinals appeared on the Bitcoin blockchain.

The Taproot wizards inscribed an ordinal that filled an entire block with 4 MB. While normally hundreds of transactions are verified in a block, this ordinal was exactly one transaction.

Advantages for Bitcoin

I have already described the disadvantages of overloading. But there are also significant advantages.

As I described in the "Miner" section, the reward for a block created is halved approximately every four years. In addition to the block reward, the miner receives all transaction fees contained in the block.

Two Challenges:

The income from the block reward decreases.

If the transaction volume decreases, the transaction fees also decrease

Since, at least in theory, Bitcoin is becoming increasingly rare, the price should rise. However, this only works if demand remains constant or grows.

Bitcoin is currently seen less as a means of payment and more as digital gold. Bitcoin serves as a store of value. As a result, transactions are declining or stagnating.

Therefore, it can happen that a block contains only a few transactions, causing the miners' income to fall further.

In the worst-case scenario, Bitcoin mining becomes economically unviable and miners leave the network.

This massively impairs the security of the network. This in turn can impair the use of Bitcoin.

With the inscriptions and the layer 2 smart contract possibilities, further applications are added to the Bitcoin network. This means that the network will be used more and thus secure revenue through transaction fees.

The more applications run on the Bitcoin blockchain, the higher the miners' income and the lower the risk of miners leaving the network. This keeps

Bitcoin secure and decentralized.

Blockchain Applications in the Real World

So far, we have looked at applications that can be used via the internet.

But these are by no means all the opportunities that blockchain technology makes possible.

Below, I will show you some examples of how blockchain technology can simplify processes without compromising the high level of data security.

You will see from the examples that there are still one or two gaps, and obviously some things cannot work like this.

After the examples, I will show you the options that already exist to close these gaps.

Cars

Data Collection in Cars

All new vehicles are connected to an external entity.

Some more and some less. According to the ADAC in Germany, manufacturers not only collect technical data such as the fill level of various fluids or temperatures.

GPS data, call data and much more is also collected. This allows vehicle manufacturers to draw conclusions about driving style, the number of users, media usage and the vehicle's area of use.

The owner of the vehicle cannot read this data and is often not even aware that this data is being collected.

The collected data is regularly transmitted to the manufacturer. At Mercedes-Benz, this happens every two minutes via "Me connect". You can probably imagine how much data is collected over the course of a car's life and what the manufacturers know about the owner.

In addition to collecting data, some manufacturers can also access the vehicle's functions.

For example, according to the ADAC, Renault can prevent the batteries of the ZOE electric vehicle from charging and thus immobilize the vehicle.

All in all, a very unpleasant situation.

I don't want to go into detail about this behavior, but it should make you think. The fact is that this data exists and is largely kept under wraps by the manufacturers.

Resale

If this collected data or at least parts of it were stored on a public blockchain, buyers of a used car could easily call up the history of the vehicle in question.

Have the inspection intervals been adhered to, has the vehicle only been used for short journeys, is the mileage correct and is there any accident damage?

This would provide the buyer with important information when making a purchase decision. The data would bring added value for prospective buyers and honest sellers.

By storing the data on a blockchain, the data cannot be manipulated and should make it difficult for fraudsters to manipulate the vehicles in terms of mileage, for example.

BMW, to name just one manufacturer, is working on this possibility.

The Verify Car app on the VeChain blockchain.

Leasing

As we have seen with Renault, Renault can prevent the vehicle from being charged.

This is likely to be similar for most vehicle manufacturers. This probably also applies to the latest generation of gasoline or diesel vehicles.

The manufacturer has the option of immobilizing the vehicle. This opens up new ways for leasing companies to collect the leasing installments.

This is certainly not a nice option and may be tricky in terms of data protection.

The lessee is a week behind with his installment payments, and the vehicle won't start until the installment is paid. Such simple if/then logic can easily be handled via a smart contract on a blockchain.

If the lessee is one month late, the towing service is automatically ordered and the location coordinates are provided at the same time.

This can also be fully automated. This means that a considerable amount of time and work could be reduced to a minimum.

Construction, Major Projects and Real Estate

For the construction industry or other large-scale projects, blockchain technology could also contribute a great deal to efficiency.

Be it in payment processing for subcontractors and ultimately in documentation.

Let's assume you are a tiling company and have been commissioned to tile the bathrooms and kitchens in a block of flats to be built. Let's say a total of 100 rooms in fifty apartments on ten floors.

In the contract, you were promised an amount X for each completed kitchen and an amount Y for each completed bathroom. You have completed the first apartment and have your work confirmed by the client.

As soon as acceptance is confirmed, you will be paid 75 percent of the agreed amount via a smart contract. Once you have completed the first floor, the remainder of your credit balance from this floor will be transferred to you, again via a smart contract.

This means that you as a contractor have a constant receipt of payment, which keeps you solvent.

The client can easily document when the respective work has been completed. This gives the client an up-to-date overview of the progress of the work and shows whether the schedule is being adhered to.

After completion of the construction work, a complete documentation of the work, the time required and, of course, the acceptances can be created, theoretically down to the minute.

In addition, the underlying plans of the work can easily be saved with the respective partial acceptance. This makes it clear at all times which plans were used in the respective construction phase, while at the same time these plans are stored unalterably on the blockchain.

This makes future work on the building much easier, as the plans actually used can be viewed at any time.

As you can see, blockchain technology can simplify many processes and reduce human error on complex construction sites or large-scale projects.

Real Estate

Yes, you read that right, real estate.

Allow me to explain how this could work using a purely hypothetical example:

You are involved in the development and implementation of apartment buildings. You have already completed all the necessary building authority applications and now have to take care of the financing and implementation.

For financing, you could now offer NFTs, each representing one square meter of living space in the new house. This means that investors with a small budget can also participate in your project.

As soon as all NFTs are sold and the financing is in place, you can start construction.

After completion, all NFT owners will share in the net rental income proportionally the number of NFTs held.

At the same time, you implement a marketplace on your website where the NFTs can be traded. You could earn one percent on each trade and thus increase your reserves for maintenance tasks. You have thus created a much more liquid market for the apartment building, as the NFTs are freely tradable.

If the property is sold outright, the NFT holders will share in the profits.

Subsequently, you transfer voting and proposal rights to each NFT holder. This gives the owners the opportunity to vote on investments, property management and other decisions.

The owners can also submit their own proposals for voting. As all NFT holders can be clearly identified at all times in this example and their data is stored in a smart contract on the blockchain, the bureaucratic effort is reduced to a minimum.

It is always clear who holds how many NFTs.

In the event of a sale, it is also possible to see at any time who has sold how many shares to whom. This means that lawyers and notaries are no longer needed, and the land registry can simply read the new ownership structure from the blockchain.

As you have seen from this example, this form can also be transferred to other objects. This is known as the tokenization of real objects. Vintage cars, works of art, photovoltaic systems, ships, and many others.

Tokenization also enables small investors to invest in assets that are otherwise only available to large investors. It also creates a much more liquid market for such items.

Supply Chains, Transportation, and Logistics

The area of supply chains, transportation, and logistics requires a great deal of effort in terms of forms, permits, and customs documents.

In addition, proof of origin or production is becoming increasingly important in trade. This applies to all types of raw materials, agricultural products and consumer goods.

Consumers want to know under what circumstances the raw materials were obtained, how the farm animals were kept, and what the working conditions were like during the production of consumer goods.

Blockchain applications can contribute to greater efficiency and transparency in all of these challenges.

In the following fictitious example, I would like to give you an understanding of these possibilities:

A coffee plantation in Africa sends a load to a coffee roasting company in Europe, which in turn sells its coffee in supermarkets.

In Africa, the cargo is prepared for shipment. The cargo is collected by a local transport company and delivered to an inland freight forwarder, who transports the cargo to the next port of transit.

There, the cargo is loaded onto a cargo ship and delivered to the port of destination in Europe.

In Europe, the cargo is returned to a shipping company and arrives at the coffee roasting plant after transportation.

After roasting, the finished coffee is packaged and delivered to the supermarkets by a transport company.

As you can see, many companies are needed just to transport the load of coffee, all of which use different systems for documentation and invoicing.

This means that every time the load is handed over for onward transportation, a new data record is created, which sometimes has to be entered manually.

Then there are all the official documents, such as for customs.

Now let's take a look at how DLT technology could help:

A GPS (Global Positioning System) transmitter and a temperature sensor are attached to the cargo on the plantation.

Every 15 minutes, these sensors send their data to a freight document that runs on the blockchain. All the plantation and cargo data is stored on this electronic freight document.

As soon as the load arrives at the warehouse of the local transport company and no excess load temperature has been recorded, payment for the delivery to the plantation could already be made automatically.

These processes are repeated until the cargo arrives at the roasting plantation.

The fact that all cargo data is stored on a digital freight document on the blockchain means that it can be read out at any time. This means that every company involved in the transport simply transfers the data to its own software via an interface.

This minimizes the risk of incorrect data entry. The same applies to customs. Customs accesses the data on the freight document and integrates the data into its own system.

As a GPS transmitter also travels with the load, it is always possible to see exactly where the load is and when it will arrive at customs, for example.

In the coffee roasting plant, all data can also be transferred to this shipping document. For example, the roasting temperature, the roasting time and the time of packaging.

This allows the customer in the supermarket to view the entire supply chain using a QR code. When was the load collected from the plantation, what are the working conditions on this plantation, when did it pass through customs, etc.?

In addition to the simplification of payment flows, administration and scheduling, there is a further advantage in troubleshooting.

Assuming that the temperature in the load temporarily exceeded a limit value, it is possible to determine precisely where this excess occurred.

The refrigerated truck could have a faulty cooling unit. It displays the desired temperature in the truck driver's cab, but in reality the temperature on the loading area is much higher.

Using the position and time data on the freight document, the faulty truck could be quickly identified and the malfunction rectified.

With this example, I wanted to show you the basic application possibilities for the transportation of goods.

Of course, other sensors necessary for the quality of the load can also be used. For example, CO2 or vibration sensors.

Other applications could also include luxury goods, precious stones, precious metals or jewelry.

Insurances

Another broad field of application is insurance.

One possibility is to pay out a kind of emergency aid in the event of damage.

Let's say you have a car accident with fender bender abroad. The details of your vehicle are immediately sent to a smart contract, and this triggers a small payment to reduce your additional costs. For example, you need a cab and have to book a hotel room at short notice. An immediate payment of say 200 would cover these additional costs for the moment.

In the event of an extreme weather event, similar payments could be made to the insured individuals. In this case, the exact weather data is sent to a smart contract, which triggers the immediate payments.

You may be wondering where the smart contract gets this weather data from.

This is where the so-called oracles come into play, which I would like to explain to you shortly.

Oracle

One of the most difficult challenges of DLT technology is the connection between the real and digital worlds.

A blockchain application can only access data that is stored on a blockchain.

Blockchains are purely digital databases that initially have no access to real data.

Weather, stock market prices, election results, etc. are data from the real world.

In the example of insurance, we need this data in the digital world of DLT applications.

An oracle provides this data.

An oracle is the link that connects the real world with the digital world, but it is decentralized and cannot be manipulated.

Below, I will show you the concept of an oracle and how a blockchain application receives this data:

The weather data, for example, is provided by various institutions.

These can be government institutions such as the ZAMG (Central Institute for Meteorology and Geodynamics) or aviation weather data from Austro Control in Austria.

This data is now collected by nodes and made available to blockchain applications.

The more secure the data needs to be for the blockchain application, the more nodes are queried. The more nodes supply the same weather data, the lower the risk of the data being falsified.

The nodes have an incentive to provide the correct data. For example, if nine nodes say that the sun is shining in Vienna and one node says it is raining, there is a high probability that one node is deliberately providing false information.

This node is therefore penalized. This works in the same way with the Proof of Stake consensus mechanism, which you have already become familiar with. Every oracle node must provide collateral if it wants to make data available.

The more collateral is deposited, the more likely this node is to be considered as a data source for blockchain applications. The amount of collateral is a sign that this node works very accurately and has therefore been able to attract many investors who provide their funds as collateral.

If this node were to work uncleanly or even make deliberately false statements, investors would immediately withdraw their funds deposited as collateral. As you can see, with a clever incentive structure, all nodes will endeavor to provide good data.

This does not only refer to oracles, you will find these incentives in all serious Web3 applications. The amount of data made available continues to grow every day.

Stock market data, weather data, sports results and election results, to name just a few, enable a wide variety of blockchain applications.

Without the Rose-Tinted Glasses

All the possible applications I have shown you have been explained through the rose-tinted glasses of a DLT enthusiast, so to speak.

In this chapter, I would like to show you the points of criticism and the dangers in more detail.

There is no doubt that DLT technology can solve some challenges and create new business and use cases.

However, this technology is not needed for any applications.

Decentralized vs. Centralized

Some, mostly dubious, influencers and many supposed blockchain experts are propagating the end of centralized databases on social media and want to move all digital processes to a blockchain or a DAG.

To put it mildly, this is complete nonsense.

A blockchain or a DAG are basically databases that store states, no more and no less.

This database cannot be changed retrospectively and cannot be manipulated by individual network participants due to its decentralized nature.

However, a DLT application is expensive, as a transaction fee must be paid for each database entry. This fee goes to the network participant who validates and verifies this database entry. You require several network participants to operate a node to create decentralization, which also costs money.

In a company, however, such a constellation would be completely useless because it is too expensive and too slow.

Let's take a company that manufactures goods. The production, purchasing, warehouse and administration departments access the same data and also produce this data themselves.

Supplier addresses, customer addresses, stock levels, shipping, accounting, etc. are data that the company produces itself. It is therefore much cheaper and more efficient if this data is managed on the company's own servers.

If this company manufactures luxury goods, it may make sense to store a certificate of authenticity on a blockchain, although this can also be done easily via the company's own servers.

With this small example, I just wanted to briefly show you that DLT technology is not a panacea that solves all supposed problems in one fell swoop. Which brings us to the next problem.

Offer Solution, Seek Problem

In the ICO hype of 2017 in particular, a wide variety of applications and business areas suddenly emerged that could be processed via a blockchain.

From battery insurance for smartphones to the tokenization of sand, pretty much everything was included.

I would like to show you two examples, battery insurance and sand tokenization.

Battery Insurance

This business idea was about insuring the smartphone battery.

When registering, the status of the battery would be read from the phone and a monthly fee would be charged based on the status.

After registration, the battery status should be read from the smartphone at regular intervals. This should be done directly via the data line without the customer having to do anything.

If the battery status falls below a threshold value, the money for a new battery would be automatically transferred to the customer's Ethereum wallet.

All transactions were to be processed in a new ERC-20 token.

The attentive reader will have noticed the subjunctive, the application did not make it.

This is an example of a solution to a non-existent problem. In times when customers can pick up a new smartphone from their mobile operator almost every other year, this issue does not exist.

What's more, you don't need a blockchain for such a service, it can also be done centrally via the insurer's servers and the payout can also be easily transferred to a bank account.

Sand Token

This ICO was about the tokenization of building sand.

This may sound partially banal at first, but it has a legitimate background.

They require angular sand to construct buildings. In other words, you cannot construct buildings with sand from the deserts of this world, as the sand is smooth and round due to erosion.

This makes it completely unsuitable for building with concrete, as the cement, the binding agent in concrete, adheres poorly to the sand.

One owner of a sandpit now had the idea of bringing his angular building sand onto the market in the form of sand tokens.

Let's say 1 kg. of building sand was equivalent to one Sand Token. The idea behind this was to create a marketplace for building sand, which was to be paid for with the Sand Token.

Since the investors in this ICO already owned Sand Tokens, the price of the Sand Tokens would increase if someone who did not own Sand Tokens wanted to buy building sand.

Anyone who wanted to buy building sand had to get Sand Tokens first to be able to pay for the building sand.

The more buyers wanted the sand token, the more expensive it became. So much for the theory.

This example also shows a solution to a non-existent problem.

It is true that construction sand only makes up a small proportion of the world's total sand reserves. But why would you need a blockchain application to establish a construction sand marketplace that nobody needs!

The price of building sand is likely to rise even without a sand token if there is a shortage. In addition, it would certainly be easier to finance the sandpit via bonds or possibly shares. This does not require a blockchain or a sand token.

These were just two examples of countless solutions searching for an issue.

I would rather not ridicule or even condemn these applications and business ideas, quite the opposite.

This is a completely normal part of a free economy and is based on trial and error.

These experiments certainly resulted in some applications that really solved a problem. These attempts might have been simply in the wrong place at the wrong time, and that in ten years' time a difficulty will emerge that was already solved in 2017.

But it seems important to me to draw attention to this. As there are still countless new blockchain applications coming onto the market today that want to make everything better.

Always ask yourself what issue they wish to solve and whether there is a problem at all. If there is a real issue, ask yourself whether a DLT application is the only sensible solution.

I also keep finding myself shifting application ideas to the blockchain that would be much easier and cheaper to manage via a simple central server

All D.A.O.?

Another trend that could be observed in 2022 is the DAO-ization of everything and everyone.

In the presentation of DAOs with a social coin, I showed you the possibilities.

However, a cost-benefit comparison must also be made here. In the example shown with the smartphone app, considerable costs can be saved in market research, as the users of the application can directly suggest changes and vote on them. This means that the issuing company knows exactly what is desired and what is not.

However, this can also be done similarly via central servers. Only when the DAO becomes very complex can it become expensive if separate software has to be developed for it.

In such a case, a blockchain application makes sense again. The required network already exists and the standards for the required smart contracts are also in place and have been tested for security and functionality.

However, there are other circumstances for which a DAO is not an option.

For highly specialized companies, for example in the chemical, pharmaceutical, energy or heavy industry sectors, it makes no sense for the end customer to have a say.

This is because the end customer simply does not have the expertise to provide meaningful suggestions.

The next point is the voting rights in a DAO.

The idea of a grassroots democratic right to have a say sounds very exciting and fair, but it harbors a great danger.

Let's take our AppCoin again.

On the one hand, it seems to make sense for the end user to hold as many of these AppCoins as possible, as this gives them cheaper access to updates and more voting rights. The more these AppCoin are in demand, the higher the price will be compared to the local currency.

But this is precisely where problems can arise.

Let's assume that a company buys AppCoins in large quantities on the open market.

On the one hand, this means that the price increases and, on the other, that the company receives numerous voting rights and can influence the DAO and thus the app.

If the voting rights were not linked to the number of AppCoin, with each AppCoin holder having only one vote, an important component of a DAO and social coins would be lost. The AppCoin could lose value as a result, as it would no longer make sense to hold several AppCoins and demand would fall.

It may therefore become difficult to find a suitable key.

On the one hand, demand should remain high and, on the other, excessive influence on individual holders should be prevented.

Another challenge can be the minimum number of AppCoins. If everyone who owns AppCoins has the right to vote, this can also be problematic.

One possible key could be that voting rights are only granted once ten AppCoins are held, and each coin represents one vote. This increases the likelihood that the holder has an honest interest in the DAO and is concerned about voting.

The upper limit could be around five hundred AppCoins. This would ensure that only interested holders participate in the DAO and that holders of larger amounts of AppCoins cannot influence the DAO too much.

As you can see, even with a DAO and the underlying idea of decentralization and democracy, there are many details to consider.

Empty Metaverse?

Let's take a closer look at the virtual worlds.

Decentraland is one of the three largest platforms with a market capitalization, i.e., the equivalent value of the Mana token, of 1.2 billion US dollars (as at 31.10.22).

The Mana Token is used as a means of payment in Decentraland and also serves as a voting right in the Decentraland DAO.

However, the daily visitor numbers in Decentraland are relatively low, we are talking about 30 to 800 visitors on average, depending on the source.

Caution is advised with these figures, as they only consider interactions with the Decentraland smart contracts. A visitor can also enter Decentraland without interaction.

Despite all this, the number of visitors is low.

On the other hand, many large companies are present on Decentraland and the number is increasing.

Heineken, Nike, Coca-Cola, Samsung, Domino's and the auction house Sotheby's, to name but a few, are represented on Decentraland.

Even the Austrian postal service operates a branch in the virtual world.

The original idea of many virtual worlds does not seem to work.

The idea was that every landowner would build a game on their plot and charge an entrance fee. This was intended to create a source of income. As hardly any people have the necessary knowledge of how to build a game and what makes a good online game, this idea seems to be failing, with very few exceptions.

Instead, virtual worlds are increasingly turning into meeting places. Here, too, we are seeing a completely normal trial and error process.

What is certain is that not all virtual worlds will survive. What is also certain is that virtual worlds will gradually move closer to the needs of the masses.

I see virtual worlds as an additional opportunity for interaction, an add-on so to speak. However, virtual worlds will never be able to replace the quality of a real encounter.

Entry Barriers

The most difficult challenge lies in user-friendliness.

For Web3 enthusiasts, it is no problem to set up a desktop wallet and use it to send transactions. Buying and selling NFTs, logging into an application with the wallet or using DeFi offers.

I know from my experience that this is far too complex for most people. It's not about liquidity mining, staking or creating an NFT, which can be considered a specialization. It's about creating a wallet and securing the seed phrase, the absolute basics.

Of course, this is also due to an understanding of the technology and a distrust of things you can't touch. After all, a Bitcoin is nothing tangible; it appears as a number in the wallet and that's it.

There are still major challenges ahead of us here.

Wallet developers must continue to lower the barriers to entry, and people need contact points where they can obtain information and support.

Another aspect is personal responsibility.

Most DLT users normally have no problem with the careful storage of their private keys and know what happens if they lose them or pass them on to third parties.

Many people would rather not take this risk. Unfortunately, there are very few institutions that offer these people an alternative.

We can see that there are still many construction sites in Web3. It cannot be assumed that Web3 will replace Web 2.0 in the upcoming years.

Rather, Web 2.0 applications will slowly integrate Web3.

It will be a slowly flowing transition, whereby many Web 2.0 applications will remain. As already mentioned, it makes no sense to want to convert everything to the new technology.

Outlook

In this chapter, I would like to introduce you to some applications and activities that are currently emerging or under development.

Entry Barriers

Smart Wallet/ Account Abstraction

A new smart contact standard was introduced on the Ethereum blockchain at the end of 2022.

The ERC 4337, where ERC stands for "Ethereum Request for Comment". This opened up the possibility for so-called smart wallets.

Smart wallets offer similar functions to a conventional banking app, as used by most people. Standing and direct debit orders are possible or sponsored transactions where the recipient pays the transaction costs.

Another advantage is the payment of transaction fees.

Until now, all transactions had to be paid for in ether (ETH), which meant that ETH always had to be in the wallet.

With smart wallets, transactions can be paid for with any cryptocurrency in the wallet.

Another advantage for the masses is that they no longer have to write down the seed phrase, the word sequence for recovery, and keep it safe.

You can designate three friends to confirm that this wallet is yours and thus unlock it again.

This is particularly helpful if your device is defective, stolen, or has been replaced for some other reason. You can easily restore access to your crypto assets.

This also opens up a new business area for companies. They will be able to offer a recovery service in the future.

NFT With Wallet

As already mentioned, the ERC 6551 standard was introduced.

This standard allows each NFT to be assigned its own wallet. To clarify:

Let's assume you have an avatar from a game as an NFT.

You use your character to collect items while playing the game. Weapons, equipment, or coins. These items now go into your wallet, which is linked to your avatar NFT. You have basically increased the value by collecting these items.

Now you can simply sell your avatar and the buyer will automatically receive all the items in the wallet as well.

You only need a single transaction to transfer the entire inventory.

This opens up further possibilities in a wide variety of areas. You can attach all your diplomas to your digital identity and document your career.

Show your NFT DID at a job interview and your interviewer will immediately see your professional background.

Artificial Intelligence

Artificial intelligence is also finding its way more and more into the web3.

On the one hand, more and more art NFTs with artificial intelligence are being created and, on the other, it helps with cryptocurrency trading and recognizes buy and sell signals.

But that is by no means all.

Artificial intelligence writes the code for smart contracts and many other programs. This can increase the security of programming.

At the same time, artificial intelligence can also check programs and possibly detect errors in the code.

We will see many more areas of application for artificial intelligence in Web3 in the future.

Marketing and Personalized Advertising

Personalized advertising is another field that is and will be increasingly used in virtual worlds.

In many virtual worlds, there are billboards. These are comparable to billboards as we know them in real life. The first attempts have already been made to display personalized advertising on these virtual billboards.

As soon as an avatar comes into view of the ad, the avatar's wallet is read and analyzed. This data is used to display an advertisement on the billboard.

The value of the cryptocurrencies and any NFTs they contain are analyzed.

Assuming you have an RTFKT NFT in your wallet, this could mean that you wear Nike streetwear in real life and the advertising is selected accordingly.

Artificial intelligence is also used to discover possible connections.

As you can see, development continues at a rapid pace and leaves no aspect of Web3 untouched. It will be very exciting to see what else awaits us in the future.

Polluters, Bitcoin and Co.

In this chapter, I would like to discuss the power consumption of Proof of Work blockchains.

My aim here is not to proselytize or convince the reader of the opposite. Rather, I would like to mention a few aspects to give you a broader picture.

The Power Consumption

One of the main points of criticism is the electricity consumption of the Bitcoin network.

This is around 148 TW/h per year and is roughly the same as the electricity consumption of the Netherlands. This in turn corresponds to just under 0.22 percent of global electricity consumption of around 170,000 TW/h.

So much for the data. (As of 2023 according to CBECI of Cambridge University)

Is It Worth It?

At this point, I need to expand a little.

The value of something is always assigned from the outside and is subjective.

If you buy a new, expensive cordless vacuum cleaner,

for example, the vacuum cleaner is worth more to you than the euro bills you have to pay for it. If this were not the case, you would not buy the vacuum cleaner.

By buying a vacuum cleaner, you will be able to vacuum your home faster and more effectively. The value for you therefore lies in the faster and better cleaning.

However, this does not mean that your neighbor has to be of the same opinion. It would never occur to your neighbor to spend so much money on a vacuum cleaner.

He uses his old one and needs it a little longer, so the euro bills are worth more to him than the more effective vacuuming of his home.

Let's take a work of art by a master. Some people are willing to pay millions of euros for such a work, others shake their heads in disbelief at these prices.

When it comes to the Bitcoin network, you have to ask yourself whether such a high-power consumption for a cross-border, censorship-resistant, decentralized and fair payment network is worth the price.

Other Data for Comparison

Of course, it's difficult to decide if you don't have any figures to compare.

I would like to remedy this here:

Gold production worldwide: 131 TW/h p.A.

Refrigerators in the USA: 60 TW/h p.A.

Televisions in the USA: 60 TW/h p.A.

Data centers: 200 TW/h p.A.

Data networks: 250 TW/h p.A.

Chemicals: 1349 TW/h p.A.

More exciting, however, are the figures for unused energy, for example from overproduction:

Electricity in the USA: 206 TW/h p.A.

Gas flared: 688 TW/h p.A.

Overproduction of renewables in China:

105 TW/h p.A.

Energy Sources

Bitcoin miners are entrepreneurs who are in competition with other mining companies.

Accordingly, every miner will try to keep the costs for mining, especially for electricity, as low as possible to generate as much profit as possible. This is the goal of every company.

As miners are very dependent on the price of electricity, they will try to obtain the cheapest electricity.

Miners have the great advantage that they are relatively mobile. They require an average internet connection and can also install the mining computers in containers.

The Cheapest Electricity

On the one hand, electricity that is not used.

This may be due to overproduction or because the energy cannot be used economically. Gas from oil extraction, for example, is a by-product that is flared off.

The other is the electricity that the miners generate themselves. Their own photovoltaic or wind power plants.

Many miners are already taking the route of generating their own electricity, as this makes them largely independent, and the electrical energy is inexpensive.

Next, I will show you another way in which the energy generated can be used for other purposes. It is often argued that not all miners use surplus or renewable energy and are therefore harmful to the environment.

This is partly true, but ignores the following context.

If a mining company uses electricity from a coal-fired power plant, it does so because coal-fired electricity is available at that location.

However, the coal-fired power plant was not built because of the Bitcoin miners, but to supply the population with electricity. The local mining companies are therefore only using the existing energy source.

It is therefore far too short-sighted to blame the miners for this.

If you urgently require someone to blame, it would possibly be the state or the power plant operator, certainly not the miners.

Can Bitcoin Support the Energy Transition?

Here is a clear YES as an answer.

In mid-November 2022, Bitcoin reached a further low of between 16,000 and 17,000 US dollars. This means that miners' income has continued to fall in dollar terms. The peak price at the end of 2021 was around 69,000 US dollars, fell to around 20,000 US dollars in 2022, where it remained for some time, and dropped to around 16,500 US dollars in November.

The value of the 6.25 Bitcoin from the block rewards has thus fallen from around USD 431,000 to around USD 103,000. That is less than a quarter of its peak.

This put further pressure on miners and forced them to work even more efficiently.

As a result, miners are constantly developing new strategies to generate more revenue or further reduce energy costs.

Bitcoin mining can mitigate one problem for grid operators and power plants.

For a power plant operator, it is most efficient when electricity consumption is relatively constant. This means that the power plant can be operated at the most efficient level.

However, electricity consumption is not constant throughout the day. At night, consumption is much lower than in the evening, for example.

In the evening, people cook, the lights are switched on and televisions are on. Bitcoin miners can compensate for these fluctuations, which also benefits the power grid as a whole.

The miners switch their computers on when little energy is required by consumers and off when demand peaks.

Many mining companies around the world are already working with power plant and grid operators to smooth out fluctuations. This service enables miners to purchase energy much more cheaply and helps to make the entire electrical infrastructure more stable.

At the same time, the effort involved in ramping up and ramping down power plant output is significantly reduced and therefore more efficient.

An almost identical buffer effect can be seen in connection with wind and solar power plants. On sunny and windy days, the electrical energy generated far exceeds demand and leads to peaks that can affect the stability of the infrastructure.

Here too, the miners switch their computers on and off in the event of overcapacity if too little electrical power is produced.

In the cases shown, mining does not take anything away from anyone or cause the power plants to ramp up their output. Rather, mining helps to keep the power plants running in the most efficient range and to protect the grid infrastructure from major fluctuations.

The first trials are also taking place where mining companies are converting the flaring gas into electrical energy to run their computers.

This means that some of the 688 TW/h that would otherwise simply be burned is used for mining. This form of energy does not take anything away from anyone either. It only uses unused energy that would otherwise be burned.

Another source of income for the mining companies is the waste heat from the computers. Stationary mining farms are starting to feed the waste heat into the district heating network. This allows the waste heat to be put to good use and generates another source of income.

On a small scale, it looks like this and is used by a tax consultant in Austria.

A photovoltaic system on the roof supplies the electrical energy for Bitcoin mining in the basement of the building. Using an air/water heat pump, the waste heat from the computers is used to generate hot water to heat the offices and provide hot water.

From the examples shown above, you can see that Bitcoin has and will continue to play a major role in the energy transition. Bitcoin helps power plants to always operate in the most efficient range and protects the grid infrastructure from major fluctuations.

It makes renewable energy sources more efficient, as they do not have to be switched off if too much wind or solar energy is produced. This means that the operators of wind and photovoltaic systems can keep them connected to the grid, even if the demand from households and companies does not actually require the power.

This generates additional income for wind and photovoltaic owners, as the excess production is sold to the miners. This makes it economically viable to further expand renewable energies.

We see that mining companies are constantly developing new strategies to generate more profits. All of these strategies contribute to a more efficient or multiple use of energy sources and are therefore climate-friendly and actively support the switch to renewable energy production.

We can look forward to seeing which strategies will emerge in the future. As I mentioned at the beginning of this chapter, I would rather not proselytize anyone here. I wanted to show you a broader picture to enable you to form your own opinion.

In the political debate, especially in Europe, people often argue ideologically without having the slightest idea about the subject.

Possibilities and Opportunities

In this chapter, I would like to introduce you to the possibilities and opportunities offered by Web3.

I have tried to show you the applications on the previous pages. I have already touched on some opportunities, but I would like to go into more detail here.

Jobs

There are many new jobs that are not based on training as a programmer or IT technician.

Of course, there are many opportunities for these professions. The demand for IT specialists is huge. Smart contract programmers, blockchain, and application developers are sought-after specialists.

However, there are also many jobs for non-IT specialists.

As many Web3 applications communicate via social media such as Discord, Reddit, Medium or Twitter, team members are needed there.

This starts with the moderators of the various platforms, continues with the community managers, who take care of the members' concerns, and ends with the support staff.

Much of this work is carried out by freelancers. As these platforms are visited and used 24 hours a day, there is a great need for employees worldwide in the areas of moderation, community management and support.

Another area is content creation, the writing, or creation of content.

This involves product updates or other information relating to the application or project. This content can be written, but can also be published in the form of videos or podcasts.

Another source of income has emerged around virtual worlds.

There is now a demand for architects and designers.

This involves the creation of 3D models. The spectrum ranges from clothing for the avatars in the virtual worlds to buildings and interior design.

My deZentrale T-shirt for Decentraland was made by a Canadian 3D expert. During a Zoom call, I learned from him that he can make a good living from it.

All the companies in Decentraland have bought their plots, but they don't necessarily have the expertise to build their buildings on them or fit them out.

This has created a market that is tending to grow and requires skilled workers.

Solutions for Companies and Private Individuals

As I have already written, many people would rather not take responsibility for their digital valuables themselves.

Unfortunately, there are hardly any banks that offer their customers this service. Institutional investors such as funds, insurance companies and similar companies also struggle to find someone to keep their crypto assets safe.

One of the few companies in Europe is the Swiss Crypto Finance Group, which is part of the Deutsche Börse Group.

Both the custody business and a crypto offering for customers are largely ignored by the established banks.

Neo-banks, crypto companies and crypto exchanges are increasingly stepping into this gap.

Neo-banks, such as Revolut, offer online bank accounts that are significantly cheaper than traditional banks.

This applies to both private and corporate accounts. In addition, Revolut offers direct integration into e-commerce applications such as Shopify, or your website with the business account.

Foreign currency accounts are also possible if you operate internationally.

As an added bonus, you can invest in cryptocurrencies directly via your account. The cryptocurrencies are displayed as a balance in the account.

It is now even possible to receive cryptocurrencies from other wallets.

WIREX takes a different approach.

WIREX basically offers a crypto wallet with the option to deposit fiat currencies. You can use a wide variety of DeFi applications in the WIREX wallet. The highlight is the debit card. You receive a Mastercard and can use your cryptocurrencies on it.

The cryptocurrency you have defined will be used for every payment or withdrawal at an ATM. You have a virtual and a physical card at your disposal.

Crypto exchanges have also already discovered the potential for themselves.

Most of the well-known exchanges offer Visa or Mastercard debit cards. You can use these cards to directly access the cryptocurrencies in your account. BitPanda, Coinbase, Binance and Bybit, to name but a few, offer these cards.

Bybit is a Mastercard with a daily limit of €5,000.

As you can see, the new companies are steadily taking over from the established banks and impressing with innovative and sensible solutions.

Things look similarly bleak in the area of investment opportunities.

There are some securities that track cryptocurrencies, iShares, among others, has launched some of them.

However, these are not the "real" crypto assets, but an exchange-traded product. Bitcoin ETFs were added at the beginning of 2024. The ETFs are 100% backed by Bitcoin, but are not yet tradable on all exchanges.

As far as I know, only one start-up in Berlin makes it possible to invest directly in properties in virtual worlds.

The investNFTGroup makes it possible for anyone who wants to invest in virtual properties.

The broad field of PfP and Collectible NFTs is also not covered. These opportunities exist for Web3 enthusiasts, but are inaccessible to non-cryptoafine people.

Some NFT projects have deposited part of their income from NFT sales in a community wallet. NFTs are now bought and resold with this balance, and the profits generated benefit the community. This is similar to a managed fund in the traditional financial world.

There are similar opportunities in the field of art NFTs. The Whale Community, founded by the pseudonym Whale Shark, also has a kind of NFT fund. The two community wallets contain NFTs worth around 75 million US dollars.

Unfortunately, non-cryptoaficiaries cannot invest here either.

Only the Liechtenstein-based company eternalyst offers an art NFT portfolio.

There, a portfolio of curated art NFTs is compiled for the investor and stored on a wallet. The wallet is stored in a high-security vault in Switzerland.

This means that the investor does not have to worry about the private keys and can still invest in art NFTs.

As you can see, there are countless opportunities for banks and financial service providers to enable their customers to invest in Web3 offerings.

I cannot say whether the refusal of these institutions is due to regulatory hurdles or simply a lack of interest.

Advertising and Public Relations

As I have already described in several places, more and more large companies are finding their way onto the Web3.

I see great potential here for advertising and PR agencies or the relevant departments in companies. All of these opportunities are largely untapped because the responsible agencies or decision-makers don't care about the topic, or rather don't know anything about it.

For the time being, it is not a question of transferring everything to Web3 and its applications. Rather, the possibilities represent a supplement to current or planned campaigns.

From my very personal point of view, companies and businesses that deal with Web3 have a clear first mover advantage, but unfortunately this is communicated little or not at all by agencies and decision-makers.

An accessible website could be sufficient as an introduction. The link to this virtual world is placed on the company website and via the company's communication channels among fellow human beings and customers.

Consultant

The problems of many companies and private individuals lie in the procurement of information.

They don't have time to deal with the topic or can't find the information they need. This is where consultants come into play.

You need competent people who have been working on the Web3 for a long time. There are countless opportunities in this area.

Consultants can specialize in areas such as NFTs, tickets, virtual worlds, financial and investment advice or decentralized identities.

Others act more as all-rounders. They present the possibilities and help in the search for specialists.

As you can see, there are many fields of activity for consultants, both in the private and business sectors.

Lawyers, Business and Tax Consultants

Another aspect is currently still underrepresented:

Lawyers, business consultants and tax advisors.

I know from my own experience that traditional tax advisors are sometimes overwhelmed when it comes to taxes on crypto assets.

I myself was lucky that my tax advisor dealt with the topic and was up to date on tax issues. Unfortunately, this is far from the case for everyone. There is still a lot of potential here.

Founding crypto start-ups is another complex area in which lawyers and business consultants are called upon. This involves the ideal company location, for example.

On the Web3, the company headquarters can be anywhere in the world, as there is no physical contact with customers.

Another important point is the regulatory requirements for crypto companies. This brings to light a problem that often overwhelms the authorities.

Crypto companies work differently to traditional companies. This starts with the payment of services. Most Web3 offerings can be paid for with cryptocurrencies, which is often difficult from a regulatory perspective.

In an NFT marketplace, high amounts are sometimes paid for NFTs, but it is not obvious who the buyer and seller are and where they live.

The amount is transferred from the buyer's crypto wallet to the seller's wallet and a smart contract sends the NFT to the buyer's wallet once payment has been made.

This can easily involve five, six or even seven-digit amounts.

This is not the case for traditional companies, where it can be very difficult from a regulatory perspective.

As you can see, these areas require lawyers and business consultants who have a deep understanding of both the regulatory requirements and the function of crypto start-ups.

With these examples, I hope I have succeeded in showing you the opportunities and possibilities for companies, the self-employed and private individuals. I am well aware that this is only a small selection.

Rejection and Negative Perception

In this chapter, I would like to address the rather negative attitude on the part of politicians and the general public.

However, I must say in advance that this is my own personal opinion. All comments are therefore subjective and sometimes provocative.

Crime

Cryptocurrencies and stablecoins are essentially an alternative to the existing monetary system and therefore direct competition for banks and central banks.

We often read that cryptocurrencies jeopardize financial stability and, much worse, are used for money laundering and terrorist financing.

This raises the question:

"Is it reasonable to carry out criminal activities on a completely transparent network?"

After all, all blockchain transactions can be checked by anyone at any time.

Chainalysis, a blockchain analysis company based in the United States, can already link transactions and wallets to real names.

Chainalysis is not the only company with this capability, but it is probably the largest and best known.

Chainalysis publishes the annual Crypto Crime Report, which analyzes the amount of criminal activity in relation to the total transaction volume on the monitored blockchains.

In 2021, criminal activity amounted to 0.15 percent (14 billion US dollars) of all transactions (15.8 trillion US dollars) in one year. Of course, these are still enormous sums, there's no question about it, and we shouldn't play them down.

But if we compare this figure with the shadow economy in Germany, things look a little different again. 339 billion euros were evaded from taxes in Germany alone in 2020.

I therefore find it difficult to believe that cryptocurrencies play a significant role in money laundering, terrorist financing and other illegal transactions.

The next question that arises:

"How can cryptocurrencies with a total volume of around 840 billion US dollars (as at 16.11.22) influence financial stability?"

In the eurozone alone, over 16 trillion euros are in circulation in the M3 money supply. The currency supply M1, all bank balances and cash, amounts to over 7 trillion in the eurozone alone.

How can 840 billion US dollars worldwide influence financial stability?

If this were the case, the stability of fiat currencies would not be in the best of shape.

I think the problem that banks and central banks have, is the loss of control. The more people use cryptocurrencies, the less influence the banks and central banks will have.

Politics

The European Union and almost all politicians, with very few exceptions, are blowing the same horn.

As I mentioned above, the amount of money in the shadow economy in Germany is already over 24 times higher than the criminal activity on the blockchains monitored by Chainalysis.

I therefore find it astonishing that the EU is trying so aggressively to regulate and restrict crypto transactions. The EU has the full support of almost all national governments and parliaments. But here, too, it is clear that this has nothing to do with lost taxes or criminal activities.

Here, too, it is about governments losing control over their citizens. However, this raises another question:

"Where does this fear of the political elites come from?"

I will take the liberty of quoting Thomas Jefferson here:

"When the government fears the people, liberty reigns. When the people fear the government, tyranny reigns."

(Source: https://beruhmte-zitate.de/zitate/1979396-thomas-jefferson-wenn-die-regierung-das-volk-furchtet-herrscht-fre/)

Let everyone decide for themselves which direction the governments have been moving in recently.

Regulation

First, I would like to mention that I have nothing against sensible regulation of the crypto market.

Sensible regulation sets framework conditions and, to a certain extent, limits the playing field on which the crypto market can develop and operate.

This creates legal certainty for all participants and enables more people and institutions to participate in the market.

However, it should not intervene in partial aspects of the market. The big problem lies in the fundamentally new way the crypto markets work and the lack of understanding on the part of the regulating authorities and decision-makers.

It seems to me like trying to stop a B-2 stealth bomber from flying over with a bow and arrow.

It must also be clear that cryptocurrencies can always be used for illegal transactions, just as is the case with all other currencies. The absolute front-runner is probably the US dollar.

Only if you understand the technology will you realize that cryptocurrencies are much more transparent than all other currencies.

Remember, all transactions are stored unalterably and can be viewed by anyone at any time.

A decentralized exchange (DEX) works via a smart contract and makes it easy to exchange crypto assets.

For example, Ethereum to Matic or USDC. There is no third party such as a bank or exchange office as we know them.

However, all transaction details are stored on the blockchain. The same applies to many decentralized applications.

So why try to regulate these applications into the ground?

Every transaction is stored on the blockchain.

Canton of Zug

I would like to take this opportunity to briefly introduce you to the canton of Zug in Switzerland.

How the canton of Zug has risen from a rural canton to a globally recognized Crypto Valley.

In a nutshell, the canton of Zug began significantly reducing taxes for companies in the last century. As a result, many companies settled in the canton of Zug. The overall tax burden is around half the average tax rate in Switzerland.

In concrete terms, this means that a single person with an annual income of 100,000 Swiss francs pays between 5.8 and 6.5 percent tax. A married couple with two children pays a maximum of 2 percent.

The percentage differences are due to the different municipal taxes.

The same applies to corporate taxes. Thanks to these low tax rates, leading global corporations have settled in the canton of Zug. Glencore, Roche, Nestlé, to name but a few, pay taxes in the canton of Zug.

Although these taxes are very low in percentage terms and lucrative for the companies, the tax revenue in Swiss francs is enormous.

As a result, Switzerland's poorhouse has become one of the richest cantons, and everyone benefits.

The canton of Zug has behaved in a very similar way in the emerging crypto markets. The canton of Zug was one of the first authorities in the world to allow payments in Bitcoin.

In a next step, Zug began to establish a legal framework for crypto companies.

Start-ups have the opportunity to implement their business model in close cooperation with the authorities.

The authorities draw attention to potential problems, such as regulatory requirements, and present possible solutions to the challenges.

In short, the authorities work closely with the crypto companies and help to solve any challenges. The result of these efforts? Ethereum, Cardano, Solana, Bitcoin-Swiss and many other companies are based in the canton of Zug.

According to a report by Netzwoche, over a thousand companies in the blockchain sector have set up shop in Zug and employ around 6,000 people locally.

The value of the fifty largest companies is estimated at 612 billion US dollars.

The situation in the Principality of Liechtenstein is very similar, albeit on a smaller scale.

Liechtenstein created a regulatory framework with its own law in 2020 and responded to the new markets.

For example, it is possible to set up a limited liability company and deposit the capital in the form of Bitcoin.

The examples shown above should give you an idea of how sensible regulation can benefit everyone.

Of course, not all that glitters is gold in the cases shown, such as Zug, Switzerland in general and Liechtenstein.

However, it shows that early recognition of opportunities and sensible regulatory action pays off.

However, this requires an open and unbiased approach on the part of the authorities, as this is the only way to recognize and promote opportunities.

Unfortunately, the situation is somewhat different in the European Union. It seems to me that there is more of a negative attitude here and attempts are being made to regulate everything down to the last detail.

It should therefore come as no surprise that the big crypto companies are setting up anywhere but in the EU.

I would like to point out that the above is my own opinion.

I hope I was able to introduce you to the world of cryptocurrencies and blockchain technology in the first part. You now have sound knowledge of the functions, the applications and the resulting opportunities.

In the next part, I will show you how to set up a wallet, how to document your transactions and a few other details that will allow you to get off to a secure start.

How to!

Now that you have a sound overview of the technology, applications and possibilities, I will show you the basic practical requirements for using what you have learned on the following pages.

- Setting up a wallet

- Tips for dealing with wallets

- Crypto exchanges

- Wallet structure

- Transaction documentation

Before we turn our attention to setting up a wallet, a few words about the different types of wallet.

Wallet Types

Crypto Exchange Account

You know that the owner of the private keys has full control over the crypto assets contained in the wallet.

You do not own the private keys on an exchange. Your wallet, or exchange account, only contains the receipts for the crypto assets that you store on the exchange.

Your Bitcoin, for example, is held in a collective wallet of the exchange and your account basically shows the confirmation of the number of Bitcoin stored.

This means that the exchange has the private keys for all Bitcoin stored in the collective wallet.

If this exchange is attacked, your Bitcoin may be stolen.

Of course, the exchanges focus on the highest possible security and reimburse lost crypto assets if the funds are available.

There is a saying in the crypto world that gets to the heart of the problem:

Not your Key's, not your Coins!

It is therefore advisable not to store crypto assets on an exchange.

Personally, I only use exchanges to exchange and pay out in euros or vice versa. Otherwise, I hold my crypto assets in my wallets.

Below you will find a rough list of the different wallets, in ascending order of security:

- Exchange account

- Browser extension and mobile phone

- Hardware wallet

- Card wallet

Browser and Phone Wallets

The wallets on your browser or phone are so-called hot wallets that connect directly to the internet.

With these wallets, you hold the private keys and have full control. However, as the wallets connect to the Internet, there is a risk of attack and loss of the assets held.

You also use these wallets when you connect to a Web3 application.

Therefore, only crypto values that you need frequently be stored on these wallets. For example, an NFT that provides you with access to an offer.

The most common wallets in this area are:

- MetaMask: for Ethereum and all EVM blockchains

- Phantom: for the Solana blockchain

- Coinbase: for all blockchains

- Trust: for all blockchains

- Exodus: for all blockchains

Hardware-Wallet

Hardware wallets are external devices similar to a USB stick.

These hardware wallets store all private keys in the device. They never connect to the internet and are therefore very secure.

If you want to carry out a transaction, you must confirm this on the hardware wallet. This basically involves asking whether you have the appropriate private key. The hardware wallet confirms ownership.

This means that your keys never leave the hardware wallet; the hardware wallet only answers the request with Yes or No.

Only buy hardware wallets directly from reputable providers. After receipt, check that the USB port is sealed! If there is no longer a seal, the wallet has probably been tampered with.

In this case, do not use it!

To crack a hardware wallet, the attacker must be in physical possession of the hardware wallet. This makes hardware wallets ideal for long-term storage or large amounts.

The best-known hardware wallets:

- BitBox: Bitcoin only.

- TREZOR: Depending on the model, almost all blockchains.

- LEDGER.: Depending on the model, almost all blockchains.

Card-Wallets

Card wallets are among the most secure wallets of all, as they are completely offline and do not even need to be connected to a computer.

As the name suggests, they are wallets in check card format, similar to a bank card.

The public key is visible on the card and the private key is sealed. This allows you to transfer crypto values to the wallet using the visible public key.

To make transactions from the wallet, you must use the sealed private key.

As soon as the seal is opened, the wallet is invalidated and should no longer be used.

Card wallets are always just one account on a blockchain. They are available for Bitcoin and Ethereum.

Only use card wallets from reputable issuers!

The Austrian state printing company is probably the best provider in Europe.

Difference Wallets and Accounts

Except for the Card wallet, you can create several accounts within one wallet.

In MetaMask, for example, you can create one account for NFTs, one just for ether and one for other coins that run on the Ethereum blockchain.

All these accounts have their public and private key.

You can also import an account from another Ethereum wallet into Metamask using the private key, or link a hardware wallet to MetaMask.

Difference Seed Phrase and Private Key

Use the seed phrase to restore all accounts in your wallet, including the private and public key. With the private key, you only restore one account, matching the public key of the account.

Wallet Setup

Setting up a wallet always follows the same pattern.

Regardless of whether it is a hardware wallet, a browser extension or a mobile wallet.

After downloading or plugging in a hardware wallet for the first time, the following steps must be completed. There are only differences when it comes to entering a password.

Setting a password. This can be at the very beginning of the process or at the end.

Display the seed phrase. This is the sequence of words you need to restore the wallet.

Checking the seed phrase

Seed-Phrase

ALWAYS write the seed phrase by hand on a sheet of paper.

Never copy/paste it to your computer and never print it out.

Both your computer and the printer could be compromised. This gives unknown persons access to your word sequence and full control over your wallet.

During setup, you must enter the word sequence again to check it. This is to ensure that you have written down the correct words in the correct order.

Once you have finished, keep the word sequence in a safe place. This is your access data, if you lose the word sequence, you will not be able to restore the wallet!

To secure the word sequence, you can write it on a stainless-steel plate or on special metal storage options. Enter "Crypto-Steel" in your search engine and you will be shown various options.

It is also advisable to store copies of the word sequence in several places. With your parents, in a safe deposit box or in a safe.

Password

Depending on whether you use a hardware wallet or a hot wallet, the quality of the passwords plays a different role.

With a hardware wallet, it provides additional protection in case you lose the device. With TREZOR, access is blocked if the password or pin is entered incorrectly 16 times.

The password is the only protection for hot wallets, browser extensions and telephone wallets. You should therefore use a strong password there.

To change the password, you must always set up the wallet again. To achieve this, you must download the desired wallet again and click on the "Use existing wallet" tab.

You will then be asked to enter your seed phrase. You can then assign a new password.

Multiple Devices

You can use the wallet on several devices with your word sequence.

As with changing the password, load the wallet onto the desired devices and set up an existing wallet with your word sequence.

You can also use the word sequence if you want to use a wallet from another provider. The word sequence is used to generate all private keys and the corresponding public keys.

This happens independently of the wallet provider. The wallet providers are only the user interface and your access to the blockchain. The public and private keys are used to operate the blockchain and are therefore provider-independent.

Use of Hot Wallets

Below, I would like to show you a few tips and tricks for using hot wallets.

I use a MetaMask wallet for this. All providers have more or less the same functions, but not necessarily in the same place.

With other providers, you may have to search for these functions, but they are available.

Basic Functions

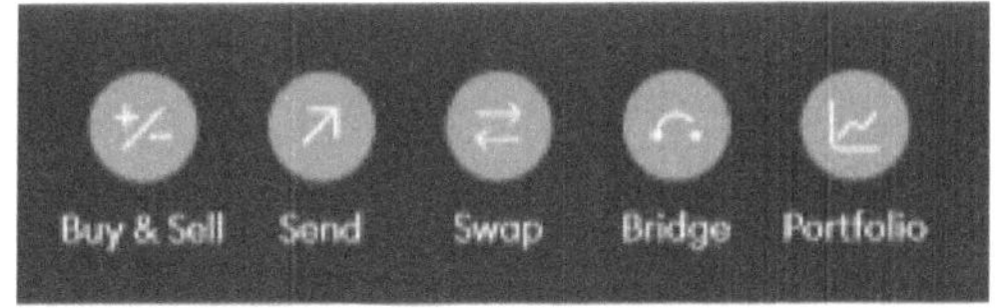

Buy & Sell:

You can use this button to buy and sell cryptocurrencies directly with a credit card. You do not have to go through a crypto exchange. However, please note that the fees charged may be higher.

Send:

Click here if you want to send crypto values.

After clicking, you must enter the public key of the recipient account. You can also select which value/coin should be sent and, of course, the quantity.

You would use this function to send crypto values to your exchange account. If you would like to transfer values between your accounts, simply select one.

CV/DCL, Nature Picture Shop and Domains, are my accounts.

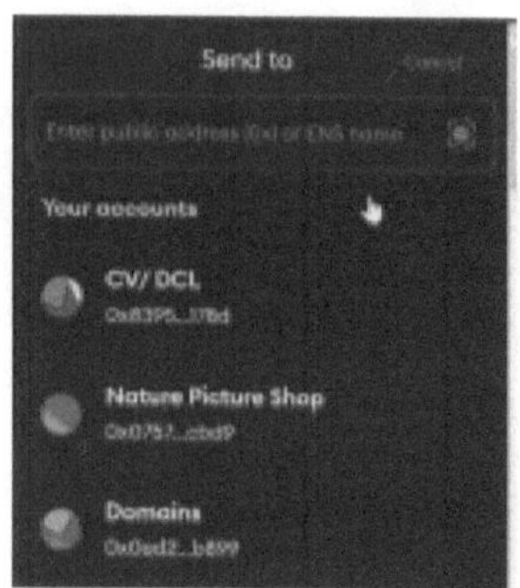

When you enter a new public key, MetaMask will ask you if you wish to give the new address a name. I would recommend this if you use this address often. The new account with the name will then appear in the list.

With the blue symbol on the right of the input field, you can scan the destination address using a QR code, and MetaMask displays the scanned address in the input field.

This helps when using mobile devices, as the input can be tedious. Please note that the transaction fees are charged in ETH.

You therefore always need some ETH in your account to be able to pay the fees. This applies to all types of transactions!

Swap:

The swap function allows you to exchange your coins for other coins directly in the wallet.

For example, you would like to exchange ETH for USDC.

Enter the amount of ETH you would like to exchange and define which coin you would like to exchange into. After entering the amount of ETH, you will be shown how much of the desired coin you will receive.

As soon as you confirm the transaction, the exchange will be executed and the new coins will appear in your account upon completion.

You require ETH in your account to be able to pay the transaction fees.

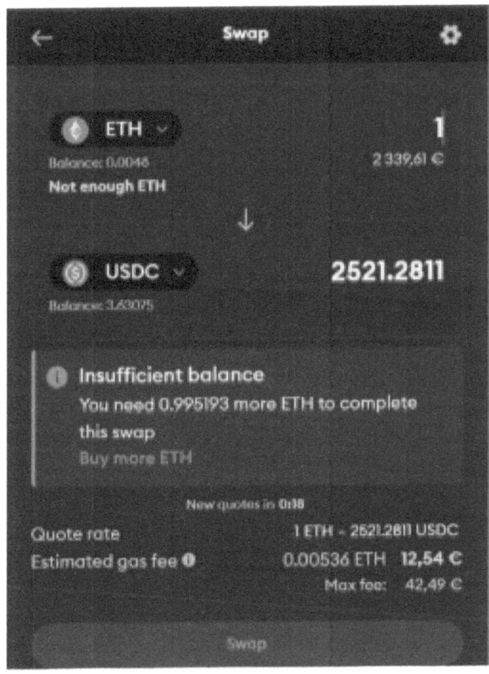

With a swap function, only coins that run on the same blockchain can be swapped!

Bridge:

You can use the bridge function to send coins to another blockchain.

In MetaMask, for example, you can switch from the Ethereum blockchain to the Binance Smart Chain.

To achieve this, enter the coin and the number to be transferred. You will be shown how many of these coins will arrive at the other blockchain. These bridge transactions are sometimes somewhat expensive.

In addition to the fees for sending to another blockchain, there are also transaction fees that are paid with ETH.

The fees for the bridge transaction are charged by the bridge operator, and the transaction fees in ETH are due for the transaction to the bridge operator.

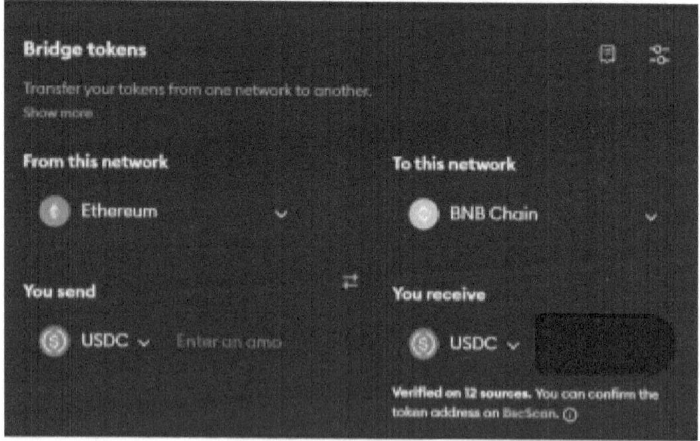

Portfolio:

This function opens a new browser window and gives you a more detailed view of your account. If you hold NFTs in this account, these will also be displayed.

Account labeling

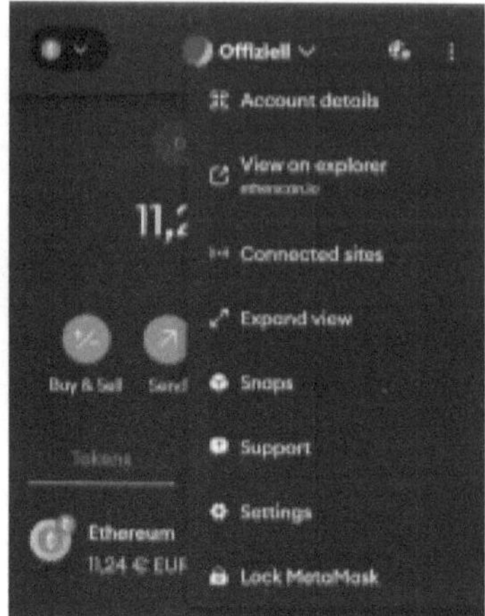

You will find three small dots in the top right-hand corner of the MataMask wallet.

Click on them to open a pop-up menu. Select Account Details and you will be taken to the page shown.

Then click on the pencil symbol (next to Offiziell in the image) and you can label the account as you wish. Then click on the checkmark and the settings will be saved.

Receive

The QR code and the blue hexadecimal number sequence are the public key for this account.

If you want to send something to this account from another wallet, enter this data as the receiving address in the other wallet.

If possible, label all your accounts. This helps to avoid mistakes and gives you a better overview.

Wallet Connect

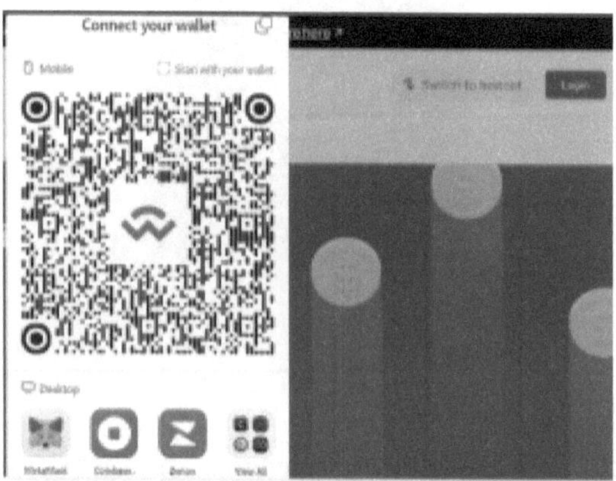

Here you can see a website with Wallet connect.

In this case, a window opens after clicking on Login. Since we work with MetaMask, click on the fox, the symbol for MetaMask, at the bottom left.

After clicking, the MetaMask extension will open in your browser, and you will need to confirm the connection.

After the connection has been established, you can use the offers on the website. (See also Token-gated access) The connection is initiated either by a login button, Connect or Wallet-Connect.

This depends on the display of the respective website. Please ensure that you do not use a pop-up blocker, as this can lead to problems with the connection.

Connected Sites

After you leave the site to which you have connected MetaMask, you must disconnect it.

To complete this, go back to the three dots at the top right and click on Connected Sites. A menu opens in which all existing connections are displayed. Please delete all existing connections!

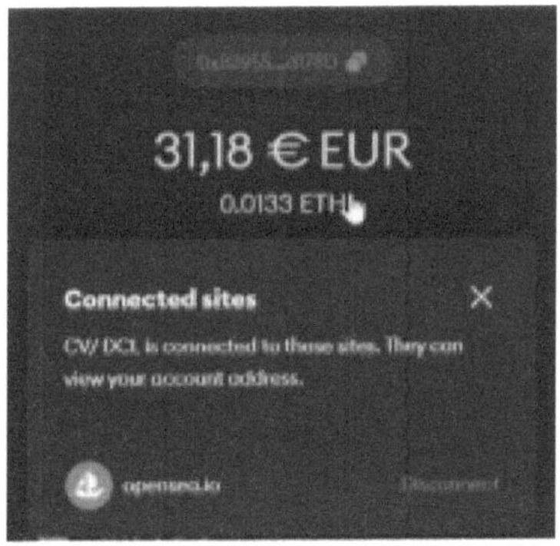

If the website you were using is attacked, there is a possibility that your MetaMask wallet could be compromised. As soon as you disconnect all connections, there is no longer any danger from this site.

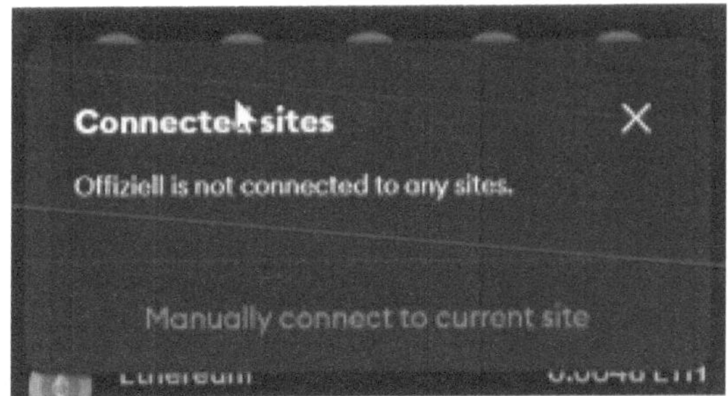

This is what it looks like when there are no more connections.

New Account

To add another account to your wallet, click on the small arrow to the right of the account name at the top center of the wallet.

This will show you all the accounts that can be operated via this wallet.

Now go to the very bottom, where you will find the option to create additional accounts or integrate a hardware wallet. You can now create another MetaMask account or integrate a hardware wallet.

When integrating a hardware wallet, click on the relevant menu item and the following page will appear:

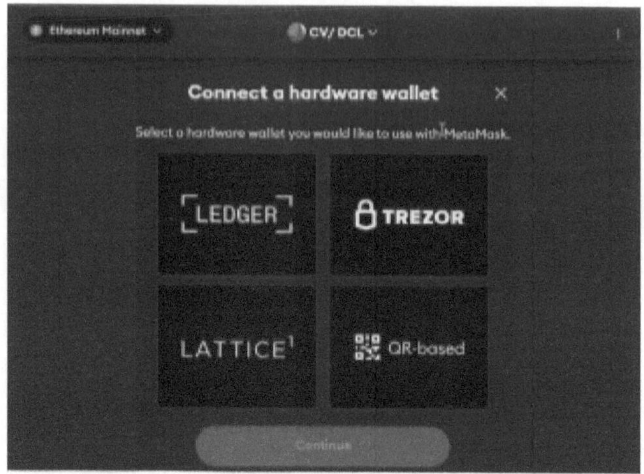

Select the desired provider and follow the steps.

You will then be asked to select the accounts on the hardware wallet that are to be imported.

After the import, you must always have the hardware wallet connected for these accounts to send transactions via MetaMask.

Security

Here are a few tips for your security when making your first transactions:

No wallet provider will ever write to you via social media! These are ALWAYS scams!

The same applies to emails from hot wallets. Since you have not entered your e-mail address anywhere, the wallet provider cannot reach you!

Firmware updates of hardware wallets always take place on the wallet's own application.

Your wallet CANNOT be blocked as long as you have the private keys! These are ALWAYS attempts at fraud!

ALWAYS check the receiving addresses.

Send small partial amounts first, when the amount arrives at the desired wallet, send the rest.

Disconnect all connections to websites when you leave them.

Use the labeling options.

Always use copy/paste to enter the desired destination address, but also check this entry.

You now know the basic functions and can send and receive your first transactions.

You will find these functions in every hot wallet. Due to the different user interfaces, you will sometimes have to search for the functions, but they are available.

Please note the safety tips listed.

They are particularly important for newcomers and will help to ensure that you do not have any bad experiences.

Crypto Exchanges

In this chapter, I would like to provide you with some information about the different crypto exchanges.

Accounts

The operation of an exchange account is similar to the operation of a normal wallet.

You will find sending, receiving and exchanging there. There are also functions for the national currencies. Depositing and withdrawing euros or US dollars. All exchanges have now designed their user interfaces in such a way that you can quickly find your way around if you know how to use a wallet.

You should therefore have no major problems.

Registration

Registering with a crypto exchange requires you to provide some information.

As the major exchanges are all regulated, they have to collect customer data. This is comparable to the details for a new bank account.

The procedure runs under KYC, which means Know Your Customer. You will be asked for your personal details such as name, address, and bank account. You will need to provide some documents that are required by the exchanges.

These are usually the following:

A scan or photo of your passport, ID card or driver's license

Proof of address in the form of an energy bill or the bill from your internet provider on which your name and address appear. In some cases, this information is checked with a short video call by a verification company.

Bank Account Verification

There are various options.

One of them requires you to transfer a precisely defined amount to the exchange. This amount will be credited to your account, but shows that you have the right of disposal over the account. As soon as all details have been verified, you can use your new account without restrictions.

Your account can only be used to a very limited extent before verification has been completed.

2.F.A.

Set up 2FA, two-factor authentication, for each exchange.

To achieve this, download an authentication app. The most common are Google Authenticator or Authy.

This app generates a new six-digit numerical code every minute, which you must enter every time you log in to the exchange.

To activate 2FA, go to the Security tab in your exchange account and activate 2FA.

A QR code and a numerical code will then be displayed. Write down the numerical code on a piece of paper and keep it in a safe place. Scan the QR code with your 2FA app and after a short time a numerical code will be displayed in the app under the exchange name.

Now enter this code in the input field on the exchange website.

If the code you enter is correct, 2FA is activated.

You will need the code you wrote down to restore it if you want to use a new phone.

The Google Authenticator now links the codes to your Google account. But, better safe than sorry.

Crypto Exchanges

Below you will find four of the largest crypto exchanges that I use myself.

Of course there are others, so choose the exchange that suits you best. Compare the costs and fees and whether the exchange has the necessary licenses.

Bitpanda:

Largest European exchange based in Austria. Bitpanda is fully regulated and meets all requirements. You can also buy tokenized shares and precious metals on Bitpanda. However, as far as I know, these cannot be transferred to a wallet. Bitpanda enables savings plans and offers a debit card that you can use to pay with your crypto assets.

Coinbase:

Coinbase is the world's largest exchange, alongside Binance. It is headquartered in the United States. Coinbase is licensed in the EU and fulfills all requirements. Coinbase also offers a wallet that can be linked to the exchange account. I have had no problems with transfers to my bank account with either Bitpanda or Coinbase.

Binance:

Binance is a Chinese exchange and is licensed in the EU. As I have not yet made any transfers to my bank account via Binance, I cannot comment on this. However, as the exchange is regulated and licensed, there shouldn't be any difficulties.

Bybit:

Probably the largest exchange in Asia, alongside Binance. Bybit also offers a debit card. I use Bybit with a business account to handle my company's internal crypto assets. This allows me easier documentation for company taxes. Higher limits are also integrated.

Now you have completed your basic setup and can move around Web3. You know the various functions and, above all, the dangers. On the following pages, I will show you a few administrative tips and how you can keep an overview.

Taxes and Proof of Origin

Depending on whether you have generated profits, these are taxable.

This is handled differently from country to country. I don't want to go into this in detail, you will have to obtain this information for your country yourself.

I aim to show you how you can document your transactions as easily as possible.

Another point is the proof of origin of funds that your bank, for example, requests when you deposit money from a crypto exchange into your account.

Keeping your wallets and exchange accounts in order right from the start will save you a lot of time and hassle. The times when the financial authorities were clueless are over.

Also bear in mind that your transactions are stored transparently on the blockchain. You have also entered your name and address on the exchange. This means that your wallets can be assigned.

Please do not try to hide your crypto assets from the tax authorities, as this can cost you dearly.

The banks are obliged to demand proof of origin if there is a suspicion of dubious transactions. In my opinion, the banks are a little overzealous and don't really like it when cryptocurrencies are involved.

Wallet Structure

To comply with regulatory requirements, I recommend that you keep your wallets and accounts separate.

This will help you with the documentation for the tax office or the bank. The following diagram is intended to give you an idea of a wallet structure without claiming to be exhaustive:

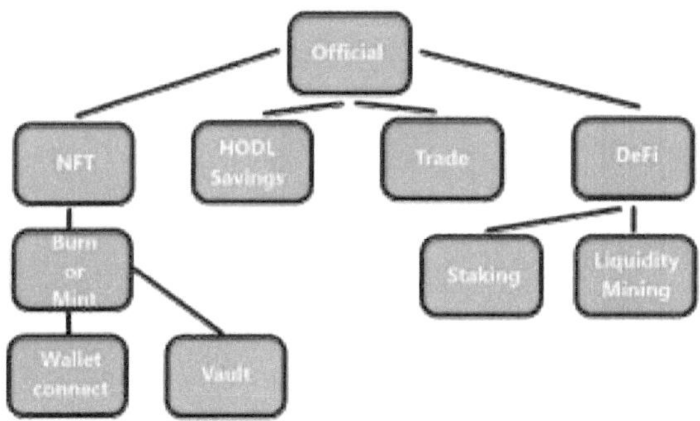

Official:

The top wallet is your connection to the outside world and at the same time the distributor to the various Web3 applications.

All transactions from and to the exchanges run via this wallet.

This provides several advantages:

You only have to save and label the exchange account addresses once. This increases your anonymity, as the other wallets are not associated with you in the first instance.

You can set this wallet address in your exchange account as the only transaction address. This means that transactions can only be carried out to this address, which increases security in the event of an attack on the exchange.

The official wallet can be a multicoin wallet, such as the Coinbase wallet or Exodus.

NFT, HODL, Trade and DeFi

You use the wallets on the second level for the applications you want to use.

The crypto values you need for the applications flow into these wallets:

- Crypto assets for buying NFTs
- Crypto assets for saving
- Crypto assets that you wish to trade
- Crypto assets with which you use DeFi applications

You use these wallets to transfer your crypto assets to the various applications and send proceeds back to the official wallet.

The two most important advantages of this are:

You know exactly where revenues and profits are coming from, and you know what tax rates apply to those revenues.

In some countries, different applications are taxed differently.

It simplifies the transaction documentation for the proof of origin of funds.

You only need the receipts of the wallet transactions involved. If you do not adhere to this structure and move crypto assets between all your wallets, you will have to integrate all wallets into the proof of funds.

Which would be unnecessarily time-consuming.

Special case NFT

The aim is to increase the security of NFTs.

Burner/ Mint:

All NFTs are bought and sold via the Burner/ Mint wallet.

This wallet contains the amount required to buy an NFT or the NFT to be sold. This means that the wallet is basically empty when it is not in use. Since the risk of a fraudster stealing the entire wallet contents is highest when mining and selling, the losses would be the lowest.

At most, you would lose the purchase amount or the NFT for sale. The other NFTs would not be affected.

The proceeds from an NFT sale will be immediately transferred to the NFT wallet.

Please note that there is always some balance on the wallet to cover the transaction fees.

After purchasing or mining an NFT, it is immediately transferred to one of the two other NFT wallets.

Wallet-Connect:

In this wallet you hold the NFTs you need to connect to websites.

It contains the NFTs for token-gated content. If you want to sell one of these NFTs, send it to the Mint/Burner wallet.

Again, you will always need a small amount for the transaction fees.

Vault:

The Vault wallet is never connected to a website.

Ideally, a hardware wallet protects this wallet. It contains all NFTs that are not used for the wallet connect.

Again, you will always need a small balance for the transaction fees.

Pro tip:

If you hold several NFTs that you require for a token-gated content, for example 3 Bored Ape Yacht Club, then only hold one in the Wallet-Connect and the others in the Vault.

The Wallet-Connect can also be protected by a hardware wallet.

Please note, popup blocker can lead to difficulties when connecting or interacting with the websites.

Depending on the browser used, the probability of problems is higher or lower.

Experience has shown that Google Chrome is the least complicated.

I hope I have been able to give you an understanding of the purpose of a clean wallet structure in this chapter.

Transaction Documentation

In this chapter, I would like to show you the two options for documenting your transactions. With the wallet structure, you have laid the foundation for the most efficient type of documentation possible.

External Software

One option is to use wallet tracking software.

You link all your wallets and exchange accounts to the application. The application automatically registers all transactions and calculates the profits or losses you have made.

This information can be imported directly into a tax report in the applications and made available to the tax authorities.

As these applications do not always link all transactions correctly, you must create the links manually if necessary. Apart from tax determination, you can also use these applications to create transaction documentation, for example to provide your bank with a proof of origin of funds.

These applications are not free of charge.

The prices vary and are based on the number of annual transactions.

I use two applications myself:

BlockPit:

An Austrian company that has implemented the current European tax laws in its application.

A tax report can be prepared at the end of the year.

So far, I have only had good experiences with the company. However, transactions need to be linked manually from time to time.

The better the wallet structure, the less manual intervention is required.

CoinTracking:

CoinTracking is a German company based in Munich.

The company offers the same options as BlockPit.

I use CoinTracking for proof of funds, as I find the reporting more comprehensive.

CoinTracking gives you countless options for sorting your crypto assets, accounts, and wallets.

My subjective personal impression is that CoinTracking focuses more on documenting transactions and BlockPit more on the tax aspects.

Both applications offer precise step-by-step explanations of how to implement exchange accounts and wallets. Of course, both cover all major blockchain networks and also enable the integration of the most common DeFi and NFT applications.

Manual Documentation

In the beginning, manual documentation should be sufficient.

This applies in particular to the proof of origin of funds. As long as you only have a few wallets and exchange accounts, this is feasible. Always assuming that you have a clean wallet structure.

The exchanges provide you with your transaction documentation. Often in several file formats. This also includes deposits and withdrawals in your local currency.

You can create the transactions of your wallets via the respective block explorer, which is basically the visualization of the blockchain.

In the following example, I will show you how this works using Etherscan, a block explorer for the Ethereum blockchain.

Your wallet on Etherscan:

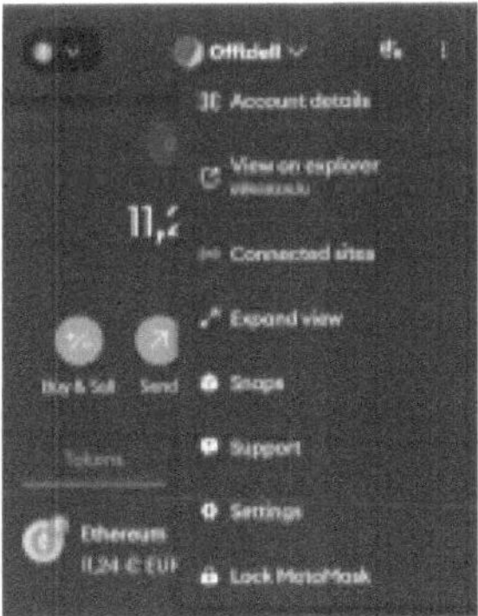

First select the wallet that contains the transactions you are looking for. Now open the menu (three dots at the top right) and click on "View in

Explorer". You will now be redirected to Etherscan and all transactions in this wallet will be listed.

Etherscan:

You will now see something like this interface:

The first thing you need to do is create an account. You will find the button for this on the top right. In the picture where it says 0knowlege.

I have already created an account, so the Sign-in button does not exist. With an account, you now have the option of labeling your wallets and adding transaction notes.

This helps you with documentation.

Labeling:

In the center of the image you will see the section "More Info" and below it "DCL/CV".

This is the name of this wallet. It contains all NFTs and transactions associated with Decentraland and Voxels.

To label, simply click on the pencil symbol, label and save.

You do this with all your accounts, including those of the exchanges.

To do this, enter the addresses in the search bar at the top right and press Enter.

This will call up the transactions of the desired wallet, which you can now label again.

You can label up to 5000 accounts in your account, which should actually be enough.

Where can I find the saved addresses??

To achieve this, open the menu by clicking on the down arrow next to your account name.

There, click on "private name tag" and the list of addresses you have saved will open.

What is the point of this effort?

The following image shows how this now looks in the transaction list.

As you can see, all hexadecimal addresses have been replaced by the clear names entered.

The example in the first line clearly shows from which wallet, Offiziell, how much, 0.1 ETH, was transferred to which wallet, 0knowlege.

Including the date and the exact time.

Different transaction lists:

At the top of the transaction list, you will find several tabs that you can click on.

These tabs describe the different transaction types:

Transactions:

Only ETH transactions

Internal transactions:

All transactions within the wallet, such as swaps token transfers (ERC 20):

ERC 20 tokens are crypto assets that run on the Ethereum blockchain. For example, USDC or USDT.

NFT Transfers:

Displays the NFT transactions.

In the following picture, you can see my ERC 20 transactions.

Here, too, it is clear to see what was transferred from which wallet to which wallet.

3.9 ETH were transferred from the "Schnipper" wallet to the "Offiziell" wallet.

I then sent the 3.9 ETH from the "Offiziell" wallet to my BitPanda account.

In the "Schnipper" wallet, you would see that I sold an NFT to these 3.9 ETH.

With this method and a clean wallet structure, you can create a proof of funds relatively quickly if your bank asks for it.

At the bottom right of the transaction list you will find a download button.

There you can download all transactions as a CSV. file.

Etherscan also offers various other functions, such as minting NFTs directly on the blockchain. All these functions would fill another book.

All blockchain networks offer a block explorer.

However, they vary in terms of user interface and options. If you opt for a software solution, a block explorer will help you to link transactions manually.

As I mentioned, it can always happen that individual transactions are not linked by the software.

You can use the block explorer to check what these transactions were and enter them manually.

The Author

My name is Daniel Müller, I was born in Switzerland in 1967 and have lived in eastern Austria since 1995.

I left Austria in October 2023 and live in Cyprus and in a motorhome in the DACH region.

I have been a self-employed event technician since 1997. I have also been a self-employed photovoltaic system installer since 2014 and have been running deZentrale.at since 2018, where I provide training for crypto newcomers, have already written two books and trade in cryptocurrency and NFTs.

Since January 2022, I have deregistered my business for event technology and photovoltaic assembly and take care of deZentrale.at full-time. This gives me time to write this book and pass on my knowledge.

I've been on the Web3 since 2016. Starting with cryptocurrencies and the ICO, Initial Coin Offering hype in 2017, I rapidly became interested in the various new application possibilities.

Decentralized identities, censorship-resistant websites and freight monitoring, to name just a few.

In 2020, I bought my first plots of land in various virtual worlds and delved deeper into the topic of NFTs.

Then came art NFTs and collectibles, and PfP NFTs.

At the same time, I became a certified blockchain professional and crypto finance expert.

In addition, I have dealt intensively with the various economic currents.

From Marx and Engels to Keynes, to the Keynesians, who have little in common with Keynes, to Modern Monetary Theory and the Austrian School of economics.

This gave me a well-founded overview of these different ways of thinking and approaches. This in turn led me to describe myself as a follower of the Austrian school and to adopt a very liberal standpoint.

Mentioned

Applications or companies marked with an * are referral links!

All information is to the best of my knowledge and belief. I use many of these applications myself.

I assume no guarantee or liability if you use one of these applications and possibly have a bad experience. You are aware of the risks and act on your responsibility.

Blockchain Networks and D.A.G.

Bitcoin

https://bitcoin.org/en/

Ethereum

https://ethereum.org/

Arbitrum

https://arbitrum.io/

IMX/ Immutable

https://www.immutable.com/

Optimism

https://www.optimism.io/

Tron

https://tron.network/

Solana

https://solana.com/

Polymath

https://polymath.network/

Polkadot

https://polkadot.network/

Enjin

https://enjin.io/

Tezos

https://tezos.com/

Avalanche[1]

https://www.avax.network/

Fantom[2]

https://fantom.foundation/

Cronos[3]

https://cronos.org/

Klaytn[4]

https://klaytn.foundation/

---

1. https://thirdweb.com/avalanche?ref=blog.thirdweb.com

2. https://thirdweb.com/fantom?ref=blog.thirdweb.com

3. https://thirdweb.com/cronos-beta?ref=blog.thirdweb.com

4. https://thirdweb.com/klaytn-cypress?ref=blog.thirdweb.com

Canto[5]

https://docs.canto.io/

Binance-Smart-Chain

https://www.bnbchain.org/en/bnb-smart-chain

Polygon

https://polygon.technology/

Lightning

https://lightning.network/

Rootstock

https://rootstock.io/

Stacks

https://www.stacks.co/

Miota/ Iota

https://www.iota.org/

Hedera Hashgraph

https://hedera.com/

Price Information

Coingecko

https://www.coingecko.com/

---

5. https://thirdweb.com/canto?ref=blog.thirdweb.com

Coin Market Cap

https://coinmarketcap.com/

Crypto Exchanges

BitPanda*

https://www.bitpanda.com/?ref=79345793961119688826

Coinbase

https://www.coinbase.com/home

Binance*

https://accounts.binance.com/register?ref=17165992

Bybit*

https://www.bybit.com/invite?ref=MX9XZX

Applications

NFT Projects

Encode Graphics

https://www.encode.graphics/

CloneX by RTFKT

https://clonex.rtfkt.com/

CryptoPunks

https://www.larvalabs.com/cryptopunks

Bored Ape Yacht Club

https://boredapeyachtclub.com/

Pudgy Penguins

https://pudgypenguins.com/

Taproot-Wizzards

https://taprootwizards.com/

NFT Marketplace

OpenSea

https://opensea.io/

Nifty Gateway

https://www.niftygateway.com/

Makersplace

https://makersplace.com/explore/artworks

Rarible

https://rarible.com/

sound

https://www.sound.xyz/

Social-Coins

Roll

https://app.tryroll.com/?state=nk8p2ndithisbo7f149gp

MintMe

https://www.mintme.com/

Socios

https://www.socios.com/

Virtual Worlds

Decentraland

https://decentraland.org/play/?position=-84%2C-12

The Sandbox

https://www.sandbox.game/en/

Voxels

https://www.voxels.com/

De.Fi

Uniswap

https://uniswap.org/

Aave

https://aave.com/

MakerDAO

https://makerdao.com/

Compound

https://compound.finance/

Yearn Finance

https://yearn.fi/

Ce.Fi

YouHodler

https://www.youhodler.com/   237

SwissBorg

https://swissborg.com/

Yield App

https://yield.app/

Mining

https://fastercapital.com/topics/the-future-of-cloud-mining-and-mining-pools.html

Masternode Staking

https://masternodes.online/

Oracle

Chainlink

https://chain.link/

Wallets

MetaMask

https://metamask.io/

Coinbase

https://www.coinbase.com/wallet

Trust

https://trustwallet.com/

Exodus

https://www.exodus.com/

TREZOR

https://trezor.io/

Ledger

https://www.ledger.com/

BitBox

https://bitbox.swiss/

Card-Wallet

https://www.cardwallet.com/en/home/

Neo-Banks, Paymentprovider, Custody

Revolut Business*

https://business.revolut.com/
signup?promo=referabusiness&ext=dezentjjx&context=B2B_REFERRAL

Revolut privat*

https://revolut.com/
referral/?referral-code=danieln5ab!FEB1-24-AR-CODE

WIREX*

https://wirexapp.com/r/Druelli

Crypto Finance Group

https://www.crypto-finance.com/

Web3 Investment

investNFTGroup

https://investnftgroup.com/

Eternalyst*

https://eternalyst.ai/en/

Tax and Proof of Funds

BlockPit*

https://blockpit.cello.so/XobHJPTo0RX

Cointracking*

https://cointracking.info?ref=0627993

Glossary

A

Account Abstraction:

ERC 4337. Account abstraction, smart Wallets

Adleman, Leonard:

Us Computer Scientist

Airdrop:

New Cryptoassets if eligible. They can be sended directly into the Wallet or have to be claimed

API:

Application Programming Interface. Connects third party applications with your website or allows data transfers between two Applications.

Arbitrage:

Usage of price differences to make gains

Asymmetric encryption

Encryption Method with a Key pair. Developed by Ralph Merkle

B

Bitcoin:

First Cryptocurrency on a Blockchain.

Bit-Gold:

Approach for a Payment System on the Internet. 1999 Nick Szabo

Block:

Basicaly the fair copy of the Transactions in the MemPool

Blockchain:

Interlinking of Blocks. each block refers to the previous block

Blockweight:

Indicates the level of difficulty used when creating the block. The harder a block is, the higher the level of difficulty.

Blockhight:

Describes the number of blocks in a blockchain.

Blocktime:

Describes the average time until a new block is created.

Bridge:

A bridge makes it possible to transfer crypto assets across blockchains. From Ethereum to the Binance smart chain, for example.

C

Chaum, David Lee:

American computer scientist and cryptographer.

He developed e-cash.

Chainalysis:

American company that specializes in the analysis of different blockchains. Chainalysis supports authorities, companies and private individuals. For example, in the recovery of crypto assets lost through theft or the prosecution of criminal activities.

CeFi:

Centralized financial applications. These are provided by a company.

CEX:

Centralised Exchange. Like Coinbase or Binance

Claim:

claim, to make a claim. If you have a claim to an airdrop or NFT, this is transferred to your own wallet by claiming.

Consensus mechanism:

Ensures that all network participants have the same level of knowledge.

Currency, Fiat:

Predominant currency system based on debt

Currency, Crypto:

Crypto token designed as a means of payment.

D

DAG:

Directed Acyclic Graph. Another way to build a decentralized database.

Damgard, Ivan:

Danish cryptographer and computer scientist.

DAO:

Decentralized autonomous organization. Company, parts of a company or projects that are managed by the community.

dApp:

Decentralized Application

DeFi:

Decentralized financial application based on smart contracts.

Degen, Degenerate:

Crypto user who makes high-risk investments without first obtaining information.

DEX:

Decentralized Exchange

Diamond Hand:

Expression from the NFT scene. Refers to holding an NFT for a long time.

Diffi, Whitfield:

American mathematician and cryptographer.

DLT:

Distributed Ledger Technology. This can be achieved through a blockchain or a DAG. Every blockchain is a DLT, but not every DLT is a blockchain.

E

E-Cash:

Attempt to realize a payment system via the Internet.

David Chaum 1983

EIP:

Ethereum Improvement Proposal.

Ethereum:

First blockchain that could process smart contracts.

Ethereum Classic:

Original Ethereum blockchain. In July 2016, the Ethereum blockchain was separated from Ethereum Classic. Since then, both have continued to exist.

ERC:

Ethercum Request for Comment. Smart Contract Standard, basically the technical data sheet for programming smart contracts.

EIP/ ERC Numbers:

Consecutive number of improvement proposals. If a proposal is implemented, a new ERC standard with the same number is created.

Equity Token:

comparable to company shares via a share.

ERC 20:

Smart-Contract-Standard or fungible, Token.

ERC 721:

Smart-Contract-Standard for non-fungible, Token. (NFT)

ERC 1155:

Smart contract standard for NFTs that can contain additional crypto values.

ERC 4337:

Smart contract standard for account abstraction and smart wallets.

ERC 6551:

Smart contract standard for linking a wallet to an ERC 721 NFT. (Token bound Wallet)

Explorer, Block, Chain:

An explorer allows you to view a blockchain. The explorer can be used to view transactions and wallet holdings. It displays all important data in plain text.

F

FOMO, in:

Fear of missing out.

FUD, spread:

Fear, Uncertainty and Doubt. Describes the process of deliberately spreading false reports in order to devalue a project.

Full Node:

Is a computer that stores and validates the entire blockchain and all changes.

G

Gas, Fees:

Transaction fees to pay for a transaction or interaction on a blockchain.

Gas, Limit:

Is the maximum amount for a transaction. This limit is displayed in advance in the wallet for each transaction.

Gwei:

Giga Wei. 1ETH = 100'000'000 Gwei.

The transaction fees on Ethereum are given in Gwei.

H

Haber, Stuart:

American cryptographer and computer scientist. Developed the concept of a blockchain with S. Stornetta.

Hash / Function:

A hash is comparable to a checksum.

Hellman, Martin Edward:

US Mathematician and cryptographer.

HODL:

Hold on dear Life. Winged word that originated from a misspelling of hold. It refers to the long-term holding of cryptocurrencies.

I

ICO:

Initial Coin Offering. External financing of a crypto project.

IPFS:

Inter Planetary File System. Decentralized network for storing files. Comparable to a cloud, but decentralized.

L

Layer 1:

Refers to the basic blockchain. Bitcoin and Ethereum are layer 1 networks.

Layer 2:

Build on the Layer 1 networks and use them to store their summaries.

Lending:

Lending your crypto assets. Basically, a Lombard loan, comparable to a pawnbroker.

Long, Position:

A long position is a bet on rising prices.

Liquidity Mining:

The provision of liquidity on a decentralized exchange (DEX)

M

Masternode:

Creates the blocks in a PoS network. Each master node must have collateral to create blocks.

MemPool:

Intermediate storage for transaction confirmations.

These confirmations are integrated into blocks by the master nodes or miners.

Merkle Tree:

Hash tree. Guarantees the data integrity of large amounts of data. Named after Ralph Merkle.

Merkle Ralph:

American scientist in the field of cryptography.

Miner:

Creates blocks in a PoW blockchain. To create blocks, it must provide computing power.

Mint:

To mint. When minting an NFT, the initial purchase, the NFT is stored on the blockchain.

N

NIST:

National Institute of Standards and Technology.

Node:

Computer / node that stores the blocks.

Nonce:

Indicates the solution to the puzzle when creating the block.

Non fungible:

Unique pieces with different values.

NSA:

National Security Agency

O

Off Chain:

For example, if transactions are processed on a layer 2 network and not on the main network.

On Chain:

Refers to transactions that take place directly on the main network, such as Bitcoin.

OG:

Old Gangster. Crypto Enthusiast with many years of experience.

P

Paper Hand:

Expression from the NFT scene. Refers to selling an NFT at the slightest price drop. Paper hand is the opposite of diamond hand.

Phishing:

The attempt to obtain passwords or private keys via forged e-mails or direct messages.

Private Key:

Cryptographic key that grants access to the wallet. Comparable to the log-in data for a bank account.

Proof of Stake / PoS:

Consensus mechanism where collateral must be deposited.

Proof of Work / PoW:

Consensus mechanism in which work must be invested.

Public Key:

Wallet Address, similar to the Bank account Number.

R

Rivest Ronald Linn:

US Cryptography and computer scientist.

Root, Hash:

Designates the top hash value in a Merkle tree.

S

Shamir, Adi:

Israeli cryptographer.

Shamir Secret:

Refers to the option of splitting a seed phrase. This can increase security, as both parts must be used for recovery.

Security Token:

Crypto assets that reflect a share in a project or company. Similar to a bond or a participation certificate. No ownership rights are associated with them.

Short, Position:

With a short position, you bet on falling prices.

Social-Coins:

Crypto assets, mostly in the ERC 20 standard, which can be generated by anyone.

Staking:

Provision of crypto assets for the collateralization of master nodes.

Stornetta, Scott:

American physicist. Developed the concept of blockchain.

Szabo Nicklas:

Hungarian-born American computer scientist. Developed bit gold and the concept of smart contracts.

T

TpS:

Transactions per second. Number of possible transactions per second.

Transaction:

Sending or receiving crypto values.

U

Utility Token:

Voucher for the use of services in a network.

W

Wallet, Card:

Similar to a bank card. The card wallet is always offline. The public key is visible on the card. A seal conceals the private key.

Wallet, Hardware:

An external device that stores the cryptographic keys. A hardware wallet never connects to the Internet. It only answers requests with Yes or No. It can also be used with a compromised computer.

Wallet, Hot:

Refers to a wallet that connects to the internet. These wallets are installed on mobile devices or in the browser.

Wallet, Paper:

The key pair is noted on a piece of paper.

Web 1.0:

Read only.

Web 2.0:

Reading and writing.

Web 3.0:

It is often equated with Web3. However, it can also be considered a technical extension of Web 2.0. Logging in with a Google account, the Internet of Things and Software as a Service are some of the developments that can be described as Web 3.0.

Web3:

Describes decentralized applications and procedures via the Internet. Enables clear proof of ownership and does not require external control bodies.

Wei:

Basically, the Ethereum Cent. The smallest unit of ETH.1 ETH = 1.000.000000.000.000.000.000.000 Wei

Wrapped Token:

If you send ETH to Polygon via a bridge, for example, the ETH is locked on the Ethereum blockchain. On the Polygon blockchain, a wrapped ETH is released. When you send the WETH back to Ethereum, the WETH is locked and the ETH is released on Ethereum. Wrapping allows layer 1 tokens to be used on other networks.

Further Information

Books

Fiat Currencies, Economics

The Road to Serfdom:

Friedrich A. Hayek ISBN: 978-0255365765

The Theory of Money and Credit:

Ludwig von Mises ISBN: 978-1620871614

The Fiat-Standard:

Saifedean Ammous ISBN: 978-1544526478

Bitcoin

The Bitcoin-Standard:

Saifedean Ammous ISBN: 978-1119473862

Blockchain function:

Blockchain Basics:

Daniel Drescher ISBN: 978-1484226032

Websites

Daily News:

Coin Telegraph:

https://cointelegraph.com/

NFT Evening:

https://nftevening.com/

NFT now:

https://nftnow.com/

Gaming and play to earn:

https://www.playtoearn.online/

Blogs

Dezentrale:

https://dezentrale.substack.com/

HiFi Bitcoin

https://hifibitcoin.substack.com/

Sources

Web 1.0, Web2.0 and Web3

Differences

https://gncrypto.news/news/web3-vs-web30-whats-the-difference/

Current Monetary System

Money

Function:

https://www.stlouisfed.org/education/economic-lowdown-podcast-series/episode-9-functions-of-money

Means of Exchange:

https://www.britannica.com/money/topic/money

Fiat Currencies:

Overview:

https://www.ecb.europa.eu/ecb/educational/explainers/tell-me-more/html/what_is_money.en.html

Currency creation:

https://www.investopedia.com/articles/investing/081415/understanding-how-federal-reserve-creates-money.asp

Fractional Reserves:

https://www.investopedia.com/terms/f/fractionalreservebanking.asp

Interest:

https://www.investopedia.com/terms/i/interest.asp

Zombie Companies:

https://cepr.org/voxeu/columns/rise-walking-dead-zombie-firms-around-world

https://cf-fachportal.de/meldungen/zahl-der-zombie-unternehmen-nimmt-weiter-zu-und-diese-gefaehrden-das-vertrauen-in-den-kapitalmarkt/

Stock Market Bubble:

DAX Chart:

https://www.boerse-frankfurt.de/index/dax/charts

Economic growth:

https://de.statista.com/statistik/daten/studie/2112/umfrage/veraenderung-des-bruttoinlandprodukts-im-vergleich-zum-vorjahr/

Real Estate Bubble:

Arise and Consequences:

https://edition.cnn.com/2023/10/11/economy/housing-market-bubble-sheila-bair/index.html

https://www.telegraph.co.uk/business/2023/12/22/ftse-100-markets-latest-uk-recession-gdp-us-inflation/

https://finance.yahoo.com/news/brick-mortar-meltdown-germanys-unprecedented-192516723.html

Politics:

https://hypofriend.de/en/consequences-berlin-rent-cap-ruling.ahn

Inflation vs. Rising Prices:

https://www.clevelandfed.org/publications/economic-commentary/
2008/ec-20080601-rising-relative-prices-or-inflation-why-knowing-
the-difference-matters

http://www.austrianeconomicsanalytics.at/austrian-economics/
monetaere-inflation-versus-preisinflation/

Weightening:

https://www.destatis.de/EN/Themes/Economy/Prices/
Consumer-Price-Index/Methods/
WeightingPattern.pdf?__blob=publicationFile

https://www.destatis.de/DE/Themen/Wirtschaft/Preise/
Verbraucherpreisindex/Methoden/Downloads/
waegungsschema-2020.pdf?__blob=publicationFile

https://www.wirtschaftsdienst.eu/inhalt/jahr/2023/heft/3/beitrag/
inflation-neues-basisjahr-und-preisbremsen.html

https://www.destatis.de/DE/Methoden/WISTA-Wirtschaft-und-
Statistik/2023/04/analysen-zur-revision-
042023.pdf?__blob=publicationFile

Currency supply and GDP:

https://austrian-institute.org/en/blog/inflation-is-always-and-
everywhere-a-monetary-phenomenon-even-in-pandemic-and-war/

Currency velocity:

https://fastercapital.com/content/The-Concept-of-Currency-
Velocity—How-Fast-Does-Money-Circulate.html[1]

https://fred.stlouisfed.org/series/M2V US-Dollar

Web3

The Blockchain:

https://bitcoin.org/en/bitcoin-paper

---

1. https://fastercapital.com/content/The-Concept-of-Currency-Velocity--How-Fast-Does-Money-
Circulate.html

Historical review:

Merkle:

https://en.wikipedia.org/wiki/Merkle%27s_Puzzles

Diffie, Hellman and Rivest, Shamir:

https://en.wikipedia.org/wiki/
Diffie%E2%80%93Hellman_key_exchange

https://www.encryptionconsulting.com/education-center/
what-is-rsa/

Merkle Tree:

https://brilliant.org/wiki/merkle-tree/

Merkle, Damgard:

https://www.geeksforgeeks.org/merkle-damgard-scheme-in-
cryptography/

Stornetta and Haber:

https://en.wikipedia.org/wiki/W._Scott_Stornetta

https://immutablerecord.com/the-co-inventors/

NIST and NSA:

https://en.wikipedia.org/wiki/SHA-2

Nic Szabo Smart Contract:

https://en.wikipedia.org/wiki/Nick_Szabo

E-Cash:

https://en.wikipedia.org/wiki/Ecash

Bit-Gold:

https://bitcoinwiki.org/wiki/nick-szabo

Bitcoin Whitepaper:

https://bitcoin.org/files/bitcoin-paper/bitcoin_de.pdf

DAG

https://academy.binance.com/en/articles/what-is-a-directed-acyclic-graph-dag-in-cryptocurrency

Blockchain-Trilemma:

https://www.researchgate.net/figure/
The-Blockchain-Trilemma_fig2_352284073

Layer 2:

https://www.ledger.com/academy/topics/blockchain/what-are-
ethereum-layer-2-blockchains-and-how-do-they-work

Open Source

Linus Torvalds:

https://www.britannica.com/biography/Linus-Torvalds

Advantages:

https://www.redhat.com/de/topics/open-source/what-is-open-source

Applications:

Bitcoin

Bank access:

https://www.worldbank.org/en/publication/globalfindex

Retire:

https://de.statista.com/infografik/25751/altersrentner-und-
beitragszahler-in-der-rentenversicherung-in-deutschland/

DeFi

Liquidity Mining:

Impermanent loss:

https://academy.binance.com/en/articles/impermanent-loss-explained

NFT

Hackergroupe Lazarus:

https://www.coindesk.com/markets/2023/12/01/north-korean-hackers-lazarus-group-stolen-3b-in-cryptocurrency/

Blockchain real-world applications:

Data collectors Cars:

https://foundation.mozilla.org/en/privacynotincluded/articles/what-data-does-my-car-collect-about-me-and-where-does-it-go/

https://www.adac.de/rund-ums-fahrzeug/ausstattung-technik-zubehoer/assistenzsysteme/daten-modernes-auto/

Car Manufactures and Blockchain:

https://www.bmw.com/en/innovation/blockchain-automotive.html

Without the rose-tinted glasses

Metaverse is anyone here?

https://www.beyondgames.biz/27417/does-decentraland-really-have-only-30-daily-active-users/

https://www.similarweb.com/de/website/decentraland.org/#geography

Environment polluter Bitcoin

https://www.lynalden.com/bitcoin-energy/

https://ccaf.io/cbnsi/cbeci

https://news.cornell.edu/stories/2023/11/bitcoin-could-support-renewable-energy-development

266

Rejection and negative perception by the public

Criminal:

https://e-cryptonews.com/crypto-crime-surges-to-record-highs/

Finance stability:

Marketcap of Crypto:

https://www.coingecko.com/

Currency M3:

https://fred.stlouisfed.org/series/MABMM301EZM189S

Currency M1:

https://fred.stlouisfed.org/series/MYAGM1EZM196N

Shadow economy in Germany:

https://de.statista.com/statistik/daten/studie/20063/umfrage/
entwicklung-des-umfangs-der-schattenwirtschaft-seit-1995/

Regulations:

Canton of Zug

https://en.wikipedia.org/wiki/Canton_of_Zug

Taxes:

https://interaktiv.tagesanzeiger.ch/2015/fiskus/steuerbelastung/

https://www.credit-suisse.com/ch/en/articles/private-banking/
steuerranking-der-kantone-und-gemeinden-so-viel-zahlen-
natuerliche-personen-202307.html

Crypto Valley:

https://finance.swiss/en/news-and-events/swiss-crypto-valley-at-the-
heart-of-the-global-blockchain-economy/

https://www.netzwoche.ch/news/2022-01-25/das-sind-die-14-
einhoerner-des-crypto-valley

Liechtenstein

https://www.liechtensteinusa.org/article/liechtensteins-parliament-
approves-blockchain-act-unanimously

https://www.btc-echo.de/news/durchbruch-im-crypto-country-
liechtenstein-verabschiedet-blockchain-act-78511/

Don't miss out!

Visit the website below and you can sign up to receive emails whenever Daniel Müller publishes a new book. There's no charge and no obligation.

https://books2read.com/r/B-A-ISZDB-XCHXC

BOOKS2READ

Connecting independent readers to independent writers.